UNMASKING THE CULTS

Zondervan
Guide to Cults &
Religious Movements

First Series

Unmasking the Cults   *by Alan W. Gomes*
Jehovah's Witnesses   *by Robert M. Bowman, Jr.*
Masonic Lodge   *by George A. Mather and Larry A. Nichols*
Mormonism   *by Kurt Van Gorden*
New Age Movement   *by Ron Rhodes*
Satanism   *by Bob and Gretchen Passantino*
Unification Church   *by J. Isamu Yamamoto*
Mind Sciences   *by Todd Ehrenborg*

Second Series

"Jesus Only" Churches   *by E. Calvin Beisner*
Astrology and Psychic Phenomena   *by André Kole and Terry Holley*
Goddess Worship, Witchcraft and Other Neo-Pagan Movements
   by Craig Hawkins
TM, Hare Krishna and Other Hindu-based Movements
   by Kurt Van Gorden
Dianetics and Scientology   *by Kurt Van Gorden*
Unitarian Universalism   *by Alan W. Gomes*
UFO Cults and Urantia   *by Kenneth Samples and Kevin Lewis*
Buddhism, Taoism and Other Far Eastern Movements
   by J. Isamu Yamamoto

ZONDERVAN
GUIDE to CULTS &
RELIGIOUS
MOVEMENTS

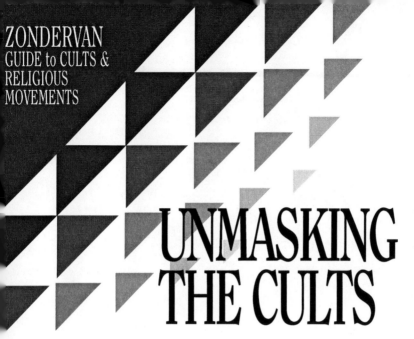

UNMASKING THE CULTS

ALAN W. GOMES
Author and Series Editor

ZondervanPublishingHouse
Grand Rapids, Michigan

A Division of HarperCollins*Publishers*

To Doug and Jean Gomes:

parents who taught me to love the truth.

Unmasking the Cults
Copyright © 1995 by Alan W. Gomes

Requests for information should be addressed to:
    Zondervan Publishing House
    Grand Rapids, Michigan 49530

Library of Congress Cataloging-in-Publication Data

Gomes, Alan W., 1955–
    Unmasking the cults / Alan W. Gomes.
        p.   cm. — (Zondervan guide to cults and religious movements)
    Includes bibliographical references.
    ISBN 0-310-70441-3 (softcover)
    1. Christian sects—United States—Controversial literature. 2.
Deprogramming—United States. 3. Evangelistic work—United States. I.
Title. II. Series.
BR516.5.G66   1994
239—dc20   94-33438
                                                                CIP

Edited by Patti Picardi
Interior design by Art Jacobs

Printed in the United States of America

95 96 97 98 99 00 / ❖ DP / 10 9 8 7 6 5 4 3 2 1

 # Contents

How to Use This Book   6

I.   What Is a Cult?   7

II.   Statistics on Cults   18

III.   Theological Characteristics of Cults   24

IV.   Sociological and Psychological
Perspective on Cults and False Religions   47

V.   Why Do People Join Cults?   81

VI.   Keeping People Out of the Cults   86

How to Use This Book

The *Zondervan Guide to Cults and Religious Movements* comprises sixteen volumes, treating many of the most important groups and belief systems confronting the Christian church today. This series distills the most important facts about each and presents a well-reasoned, cogent Christian response. The authors in this series are highly qualified, well-respected professional Christian apologists with considerable expertise on their topics.

We have designed the structure and layout to help you find the information you need as quickly as possible. All the volumes are written in outline form, which allows us to pack substantial content into a short book. With some exceptions, each book contains, first, an introduction to the cult, movement, or belief system. The introduction gives a brief history of the group, its organizational structure, and vital statistics such as membership. Second, the theology section is arranged by doctrinal topic, such as God, Christ, sin, and salvation. The movement's position is set forth objectively, primarily from its own official writings. The group's teachings are then refuted point by point, followed by an affirmative presentation of what the Bible says about the doctrine. The third section is a discussion of witnessing tips. While each witnessing encounter must be handled individually and sensitively, this section provides some helpful general guidelines, including both dos and don'ts. The fourth section contains annotated bibliographies, listing works by the groups themselves and books written by Christians in response. Fifth, each book has a parallel comparison chart, with direct quotations from the cultic literature in the left column and the biblical refutation on the right. Some of the books conclude with a glossary.

One potential problem with a detailed outline is that it is easy to lose one's place in the overall structure. Therefore, we have provided graphical "signposts" at the top of the odd numbered pages. Functioning like a "you are here" map in a shopping mall, these graphics show your place in the outline, including the sections that come before and after your current position. (Those familiar with modern computer software will note immediately the resemblance to a "drop-down" menu bar, where the second-level choices vary depending on the currently selected main menu item.) In the theology section we have also used "icons" in the margins to make clear at a glance whether the material is being presented from the cultic or Christian viewpoint. For example, in the Mormonism volume the sections presenting the Mormon position are indicated with a picture resembling the angel Moroni in the margin; the biblical view is shown by a drawing of the Bible.

We hope you will find these books useful as you seek "to give an answer to everyone who asks you to give the reason for the hope that you have" (1 Peter 3:15).

—Alan W. Gomes, Ph.D.
Series Editor

Part I:
What Is a Cult?

I. The Origin of the Word *Cult*

A. *Our English word* cult *comes from the Latin word* cultus, *which is a form of the verb* colere, *meaning "to worship or give reverence to a deity."*[1]

B. Cultus *was a general word for worship, regardless of the particular god in question.*

   1. The Vulgate, a Latin translation of the Bible, uses the word in the general sense of worship, regardless of the deity in view. For example, in Acts 17 it is used both of the worship of false gods (v. 23) and of the true God (v. 25).

   2. The word is also used in Christian Latin texts that speak of the worship of the one true God.[2]

C. *It is understandable, then, that the word* cult *would naturally be applied to a religious group of people, but this general meaning is too broad for the present purpose.*

II. The Preferred Definition of a Cult

Throughout this book we will be using the word *cult* in a very specific, precise way.

A. *The Preferred Definition*

A cult of Christianity is a group of people, which claiming to be Christian, embraces a particular doctrinal system taught by an individual leader, group of leaders, or organization, which (system) denies (either explicitly or implicitly) one or more of the central doctrines of the Christian faith as taught in the sixty-six books of the Bible.

B. *Key Features of the Preferred Definition*

   1. "A cult of Christianity..."

     a. A cult is a group that deviates doctrinally from a "parent" or "host" religion; that is, cults grow out of and deviate from a previously established religion.

---

[1]See Charlton T. Lewis and Charles Short, *A Latin Dictionary* (Oxford: Oxford University Press, 1879; impression of 1984), s.v. "colo," 370.

[2]I.e., in early, medieval, and Reformation-era theological works.

    b. Although the focus of this book is on cults of Christianity, non-Christian religions (e.g., world religions) have had cults arise from them as well.

        (1) Cults of Islam include the Sufis and the Nation of Islam.[3] While these groups claim to be Muslim, they deviate fundamentally from the teaching of Islam, from which they are derived.[4]

        (2) Cults of Hinduism include Hare Krishna, Self-Realization Fellowship, and Vivekananda.

    c. I have deliberately chosen the expression "cult of Christianity" in preference to the term "Christian cult."

        (1) Phrases such as "Christian cult" or "cultic Christian groups" are confusing because they send mixed signals.

        For most Christians, the word *cult* refers to a group that is non-Christian. Therefore, the expression "Christian cult" is an oxymoron.

        (2) The expression "cult of Christianity" makes a clear distinction between Christianity and cults as well as highlighting the derivative nature of cults.

2. "... is a group of people ..."

    a. One individual with unorthodox views does not constitute a cult.

    An individual with unorthodox theology is a *heretic*,[5] but he or she must gain a following before we can meaningfully speak of a cult.

    b. There is no other prescribed size, however, which must be reached before a group qualifies as a cult.

        (1) Some cults are quite small, having only a handful of followers, while other cults number into the millions.[6]

        (2) Some cults that have started with very few members have grown into the millions (e.g., Mormonism), while others that at one time had significant followings have become all but extinct (e.g., the Shakers).

3. "... claiming to be Christian ..."

    a. It is important to make a distinction between groups that claim to be Christian and those that make no such profession.[7]

        (1) For example, it would not be meaningful to speak of Islam as a cult of Christianity since it makes no claim to be Christian.

---

[3]Popularly known as the Black Muslims.

[4]George A. Braswell, *Understanding Sectarian Groups in America*, rev. ed. (Nashville: Broadman, 1994), 280.

[5]See Part I, section IV.C.

[6]See the statistics listed in Part II, section II below.

[7]Walter Martin agrees that cults "continue to insist that they are entitled to be classified as Christian" (Walter R. Martin, *Kingdom of the Cults*, rev. ed. [Minneapolis: Bethany Fellowship, 1985], 11). Martin, however, sometimes applied the term *cult* to groups that make no such claim (e.g., the New Age movement). See also Gordon Lewis, *Confronting the Cults* (1966; reprint, Grand Rapids: Baker, 1975), 3.

Indeed, Muslims are generally anti-Christian. Islam is a world religion that opposes Christianity, but it is not a cult.

(2) Jehovah's Witnesses and Mormons, however, do qualify as cults of Christianity because they claim to be Christian—indeed, to be the only true Christian group on earth.

b. Note: A group that admits it is not Christian is not somehow innocuous simply because it is not a cult of Christianity.

(1) All belief systems and worldviews that deny the gospel are false, and therefore lead men and women away from the true God of the Bible.

(2) The point is that not all false belief systems are wrong in the same way: Cults are false in their claim to be true representations of Christianity, while avowedly non-Christian religions are false in their denial of Christianity.

c. The distinction between cults of Christianity and openly non-Christian belief systems is not merely academic. On a practical level, one approaches a member of a cult differently from a person who is hostile to the very notion of the Christian faith.

4. "... who embrace a particular doctrinal system ..."

a. A group must hold to a set of religious doctrinal beliefs (e.g., about God, sin, salvation) to qualify as a cult.

b. A group that makes no religious statements whatever—even if eccentric in other respects—is not a cult.

For example, imagine a lodge whose members dress up each Thursday evening in moose antlers and lederhosen. The lodge president calls the meeting to order by blowing on an enormous curved horn. After reading the minutes from the previous week, members play a rousing game of bingo for two hours. The meeting closes with the lodge anthem ("a moose is kind, thrifty, and cheerful to everyone he meets"), and the members return home. Now, if our imaginary lodge makes no statements about God, sin, salvation, the afterlife, etc., then such a group is not even a religion, much less a false religion or cult.[8]

c. In saying that the group embraces a doctrinal "system," this does not mean that the system must be highly complex, sophisticated, or thorough.

(1) The complexity of cultic belief systems varies considerably from group to group.

(2) For example, the Watchtower Society espouses a relatively comprehensive system of doctrine, while the Children of God

---

[8]Note that some lodges *are* religious, such as the Masons. See the *Masonic Lodge* volume in this series.

are less systematic and comprehensive in their belief system.[9] Both groups, however, hold a belief system, and one contrary to the Christian faith.

5. "... taught by an individual leader, group of leaders, or organization ..."

   a. Some cults, such as the Children of God, the Unification Church, and the Branch Davidians, look to a strong, authoritarian "prophet" as the source of truth.

   b. In other cults, authority resides in a group of leaders or an organization. For example, the Jehovah's Witnesses claim that the Watchtower Society's Governing Body is the "faithful and discreet slave," who dispenses "doctrinal food in due season."[10]

6. "... which (system) denies (either explicitly or implicitly) one or more of the central doctrines of the Christian faith. ..."[11]

   a. "Central doctrines" of the Christian faith are those doctrines that make the Christian faith *Christian* and not something else.

     (1) The meaning of the expression "Christian faith" is not like a wax nose, which can be twisted to mean whatever the speaker wants it to mean.

     (2) The Christian faith is a definite system of beliefs with definite content (Jude 3).

     (3) Certain Christian doctrines constitute the core of the faith.

     Central doctrines include the Trinity, the deity of Christ, the bodily resurrection, the atoning work of Christ on the cross, and salvation by grace through faith. These doctrines so comprise the essence of the Christian faith that to remove any of them is to make the belief system non-Christian.

     (4) Scripture teaches that the beliefs mentioned above are of central importance (e.g., Matt. 28:19; John 8:24; 1 Cor. 15; Eph. 2:8–10).

     (5) Because these central doctrines define the character of Christianity, one cannot be saved and deny these.

---

[9]The exact status of the Children of God is questionable. While their numbers both in the U.S. and abroad have dwindled significantly, there is evidence that the group is making a comeback. I recently received a report from Eastern Europe indicating that they are actively proselytizing there. Their current activities are discussed by Joe Maxwell, "News Watch: Children of God Revamp Image, Face Renewed Opposition," *Christian Research Journal* (Fall 1993): 5-6, 41. Children of God leader Moses David, who had dropped out of sight in recent years, is reported to have died in November 1994 at age 75. Note that the Children of God have changed their name several times; their most recent name is "The Family." I shall continue to refer to them as the Children of God because this is the name by which they are most well known.

[10]Though the Watchtower Society does have a president (currently Milton Henschel), the prophetic role of the Governing Body is emphasized far more than the individual authority of the president. Earlier in Watchtower history, authority did tend to center around its founder, Charles Taze Russell, and in his immediate successor, Joseph Franklin Rutherford.

[11]Note Walter Martin's statement: "Cultism, in short, is *any major deviation from orthodox Christianity relative to the cardinal doctrines of the Christian faith*" (Walter R. Martin, *Rise of the Cults* [Santa Ana, Calif.: Vision House, 1977], 11 [emphasis his]).

(6) Central doctrines should not be confused with peripheral issues, about which Christians may legitimately agree to disagree.

Peripheral (i.e., non-essential) doctrines include such issues as the timing of the tribulation, the method of baptism, or the structure of church government. For example, one can be wrong about the identity of "the spirits in prison" (1 Peter 3:19) or about the timing of the rapture and still go to heaven, but one cannot deny salvation by grace or the deity of Christ (John 8:24) and be saved.

(7) All Christian denominations—whether Roman Catholic, Eastern Orthodox, or Protestant—agree on the essential core. The relatively minor disagreements between genuinely Christian denominations, then, cannot be used to argue that there is no objectively recognized core of fundamental doctrine which constitutes the Christian faith.[12]

b. Cults deny at least one central doctrine of the Christian faith.

(1) Denial of even one central doctrine is enough to make the belief system cultic.

(2) Cults typically deny more than one central doctrine.

This is hardly surprising since one's interpretation of a particular doctrine affects other doctrines in the system. For example, if a group denies that people need salvation from sin, it is also likely that it redefines Christ's atoning death on the cross accordingly.

c. Some cults *explicitly* deny central doctrines of the Christian faith.

(1) The Jehovah's Witnesses vehemently deny the doctrine of the Trinity (see their widely circulated booklet, *Should You Believe in the Trinity?* which argues against the doctrine).[13]

(2) Victor Paul Wierwille, founder of The Way International, wrote a book entitled *Jesus Christ Is Not God.*

d. Other cults *implicitly* deny central doctrines.

(1) Some cults give the impression of orthodoxy, but have so redefined terminology that the doctrine is orthodox in name only.[14]

(2) For example, Mormons speak of their "Heavenly Father," as do Christians, but their Heavenly Father is really an exalted man, not the God of the Bible.[15]

---

[12]I am not denying that there are wide differences of opinion between different denominations on numerous issues. My point is that however much Christian denominations may disagree, on core Christian teaching (e.g., Trinity, bodily resurrection, etc.) there is agreement.

[13]The volume on Jehovah's Witnesses in this series, by Robert M. Bowman, Jr., gives solid answers to the Watchtower objections against the Trinity. Bowman has also countered this particular Watchtower booklet with his *Why You Should Believe in the Trinity* (Grand Rapids: Baker, 1989).

[14]The problem of redefining terminology is discussed in Part III, section II.F.

[15]Journal of Discourses 6:3 states, "God himself was once as we are now, and is an exalted Man."

7. "... as taught in the sixty-six books of the Bible."
   a. Some cults add to the revelation of Scripture. They may do this through prophecies or by adding new books to the Bible.[16]
   b. The sixty-six books of the Bible are the only truly inspired writings from which one may derive Christian teaching.
      (1) These constitute the canon, meaning "rule or standard," against which all doctrines must be measured.[17]
      (2) The canon is closed, meaning that no additional books may be added to it. The faith has been "once for all entrusted to the saints" (Jude 3).

III. Answers to Possible Objections to the Preferred Definition of a Cult

A. *Objection #1: We should use the word* cult *but define it sociologically.*

1. Defining Cults Sociologically
   a. Sociological definitions "include consideration of such factors as authoritarian leadership patterns, loyalty and commitment mechanisms, lifestyle characteristics, [and] conformity patterns (including the use of various sanctions in connection with those members who deviate)."[18]
   b. As historian Ruth Tucker observes, "Sociologists have tended to define cults more in terms of lifestyle, proselytizing practices, and authoritarian leadership, rather than in terms of belief or by any standard of orthodoxy."[19]
   c. In sociological definitions, the focus is on practices that fall outside the norms of the society in which the group is found.

2. Some Suggested Sociological Definitions
   a. Charles Braden

      "A cult ... is any religious group which differs significantly in some one or more respects as to belief or practice, from those religious groups which are regarded as the normative expressions of religion in our total culture."[20]

---

[16]See discussion in Part III, section II.E.

[17]The biblical canon is not an arbitrary selection of books but was determined by objective criteria. A discussion of the canon goes beyond the scope of this book. For further study see F. F. Bruce, *The Canon of Scripture* (Downers Grove, Ill.: InterVarsity Press, 1988); Donald A. Carson and John D. Woodbridge, eds., *Hermeneutics, Authority, and Canon* (Grand Rapids: Zondervan, 1986).

[18]Ronald Enroth, "What Is a Cult?" in *A Guide to Cults and New Religions*, ed. Ronald Enroth (Downers Grove, Ill.: InterVarsity Press: 1983), 14.

[19]Ruth A. Tucker, *Another Gospel* (Grand Rapids: Zondervan, 1989), 16-17.

[20]Charles Braden, quoted in Martin, *Kingdom of the Cults* (Minneapolis: Bethany Fellowship, 1965), 11. Unless otherwise noted, all subsequent citations of this work are from the 1985 edition.

b. John Lofland

Cults are "little groups" that break off from the "conventional consensus and espouse very different views of the real, the possible, and the moral."[21]

c. Ruth A. Tucker

"A 'cult' is a religious group that has a 'prophet'-founder called of God to give a special message not found in the Bible itself, often apocalyptic in nature and often set forth in 'inspired' writings. In deference to this charismatic figure or these 'inspired' writings the style of leadership is authoritarian and there is frequently an exclusivistic outlook supported by a legalistic lifestyle and persecution mentality. . . . It is the attribute of a prophet-founder that very distinctly separates cults from denominations."[22]

d. James T. Richardson

"A cult is usually defined as a small informal group lacking a definite authority structure, somewhat spontaneous in its development (although often possessing a somewhat charismatic leader or group of leaders), transitory, somewhat mystical and individualistically oriented, and deriving its inspiration and ideology from outside the predominant religious culture."[23]

e. Ronald Enroth

"Cults are defined as religious organizations that tend to be outside the mainstream of the dominant religious forms of any given society."[24]

3. Problems with Sociological Definitions

a. Sociological definitions are *relativistic*.

(1) In the above definitions, cults are seen as groups outside the norms of society.

(2) Since society's norms are constantly changing (and often for the worse), it follows that what is not considered cultic today may be tomorrow and vice versa.

b. Sociological definitions are *imprecise and subjective*.

(1) Referring to the definitions in section 2 above, notice the subjective "qualifiers" that render these definitions of questionable value.

---

[21] John Lofland, cited in Enroth, "What Is a Cult?" 14.

[22] Tucker, *Another Gospel*, 16, 24.

[23] James T. Richardson, "An Oppositional and General Conceptualization of Cult," *Annual Review of the Social Sciences of Religion* (1978), cited in James T. Richardson, "Definitions of Cult: From Sociological-Technical to Popular–Negative," *Review of Religious Research* 34, no. 4 (June 1993): 349. Richardson has since advocated abandoning the term *cult* "because of its confused and negatively connoted meaning in contemporary society" (348).

[24] Ronald Enroth, *Youth, Brainwashing, and the Extremist Cults* (Grand Rapids: Zondervan, 1977), 168. Although this is an older work, it has been and remains a very influential book. See J. Gordon Melton, *Encyclopedic Handbook of Cults in America*, rev. ed. (New York: Garland, 1992), 336.

13

For example, the above definitions say that cults:

(a) "differ significantly" from mainstream religion (how much difference is "significant"?);

(b) espouse "very different views" (when does the view change from "different" to "very different"?);

(c) are "often apocalyptic in nature" (how often?);

(d) are "somewhat spontaneous" in their development (is "somewhat spontaneous" an oxymoron?);

(e) possess "a somewhat charismatic leader" (how many notches above "boring" is "somewhat charismatic"?); and

(f) "tend to be outside the mainstream" (what about those that do not fit this "tendency"—are they still cults?).

(2) Even when qualifiers are not given, application of the characteristics is often subjective.

For example, many sociological definitions of cults list "authoritarianism," but who decides what is authoritarian? Are Christians "authoritarian" when they say that believers should submit to church leaders (Heb. 13:17), that wives should submit to their husbands (Eph. 5:22, 24), and that children should obey their parents (Eph. 6:1)?

(3) Sociological definitions sometimes set forth diametrically opposed characteristics as cultic "hallmarks."

Tucker states that a cult has a "prophet-founder" who functions as a legalistic, authoritarian leader. Richardson, however, stated that cults are informal groups, lack a definite authority structure, have "somewhat charismatic" leaders, and are "individualistically oriented." Richardson's definition can hardly be reconciled with other definitions stressing blind conformity to "totalistic" authoritarian structures.

B. Objection #2: The word *cult* is so emotionally loaded that it should be avoided altogether.

1. The word *cult* carries negative social connotations in many people's minds, particularly as a result of popular media exposure.

a. As sociologists Dick Anthony and Thomas Robbins have stated, "*Cult* evokes occultism and the image of men wearing hoods and performing secret rituals in cellars. These unsavory associations to the term *cult* have been exploited at the expense of linguistic precision by the anticult movement."[25]

b. The word *cult* may conjure up pictures of zombie-like Moonies with glazed eyes who sell flowers in a supermarket parking lot, or chant-

---

[25]Dick Anthony and Thomas Robbins, "New Religions, Families, and 'Brainwashing,'" in *In Gods We Trust: New Patterns of Religious Pluralism in America*, ed. Thomas Robbins and Dick Anthony (New Brunswick, N.J.: Rutgers/Transaction Books, 1981), 265.

ing Krishna devotees in saffron robes, or violent megalomaniacs, such as Jim Jones and David Koresh, who lead an army of brainwashed automatons to their tragic deaths.[26]

2. Those who oppose the word *cult* say that it is used simply for the purpose of name calling.

a. The word *cult* is tossed around too freely by Christians and the media alike.

b. Sometimes Christians label any group a cult whose theology or practice differs from their own.[27]

c. Secular authorities on cults, sometimes driven by an anti-religious bias, cavalierly lump Campus Crusade for Christ with Scientology, Hare Krishna, and the Unification Church.[28]

In such cases, use of the word "reflects more on the speaker's attitude than on the subject being spoken about."[29]

3. Because of the unsavory associations connected with the word *cult*, some sociologists advocate abandoning the word in favor of more relativistic, value-neutral language.

a. "Because the term 'cults' has acquired a negative connotation some sociologists have adopted others, such as 'new religions,' 'new religious movements,' 'alternative religions,' 'alternative groups,' 'alternative faiths,' and 'emergent religions.'"[30]

b. Since sociology describes outward behavior evaluated against the ever-changing standard of culture, these new labels more clearly reflect the relativistic judgments sociology can make. Thus, sociologists should abandon the word *cult* and stick to labels such as these, which more accurately reflect the boundaries of their discipline.

4. On the other hand, I believe the word *cult* should be retained and used according to the preferred definition given in this book (refer to II.A. above).

a. The word *cult* has an established history of usage, long before the secular media or social sciences got hold of it.

b. Note that historically *cult* has been a *religious* term, not a sociological or psychological one (see I above).

---

[26]The issue of alleged cultic brainwashing is treated in Part IV, section III below.

[27]Tucker, speaking facetiously, gives this definition of a cult: "A cult is someone else's religious group that does not agree with mine" (Tucker, *Another Gospel*, 15).

[28]For example, Flo Conway and Jim Siegelman, *Snapping: America's Epidemic of Sudden Personality Change* (Philadelphia: Lippincott, 1978), 56.

[29]Tucker, *Another Gospel*, 15.

[30]Kenneth R. Samples et al., *Prophets of the Apocalypse: David Koresh and Other American Messiahs* (Grand Rapids: Baker, 1994), 160. Richardson surveys this changing terminology among sociologists and advocates its acceptance. See his "Definitions of Cult: From Sociological-Technical to Popular-Negative," 352–53, 355.

    c. The term *cult* suggests an absolute standard of evaluation, which sociology—by its nature—cannot provide. It is therefore well suited to describe theological heterodoxy, which is determined by an absolute, objective, and unchanging standard.

C. *Objection #3: There is no need to label religious groups at all.*

  1. In response to this objection, note that labels, when applied objectively, can be exceedingly helpful.

    a. A label is a shorthand way of indicating that a particular thing has certain "defining characteristics," which make it what it is.

    b. The groups to which we shall affix the label *cult* do share certain core characteristics—most notably a denial of historic Christian orthodoxy.

    c. Use of a single label does not imply that all cults are identical in every particular.

  2. Labeling a group is not (or should not be) a form of name calling or poking fun.

    a. The purpose here is objective classification.

    b. Of course, some or even many cults may have unsavory aspects about them, but that must be determined on a case-by-case basis.

IV. Words and Concepts Related to the Word *Cult*

A. *False Religion and False Belief System*

  1. A false religion or false belief system is any system of belief that opposes the central teachings of the Christian faith.

  2. While all cults of Christianity are also false religions, not all false religions are cults of Christianity because not all religions claim to be Christian.

B. *Occult*

  1. The word *occult* comes from the Latin *occultus*, which means "hidden" or "secret."

  2. As Mather and Nichols point out, "The study of the occult is generally classified into three different areas: (1) spiritism, (2) fortune-telling, and (3) magic."[31]

  3. Occultic practices may include the use of accessories such as ouija boards and tarot cards.

  4. Although cults should not be confused with the occult (as many people do), some cults and cult founders do engage in occultic practices (e.g., the Children of God, Emanuel Swedenborg [founder of the Church of New Jerusalem], and the Unification Church).[32]

---

[31]George A. Mather and Larry A. Nichols, *Dictionary Of Cults, Sects, Religions and the Occult* (Grand Rapids: Zondervan, 1993), 212.

[32]See the discussion in Part III, section II.Q.

C. Heresy

1. *Heresy* comes from the Greek word *hairesis,* which means "choice" or "thing chosen."

2. When used in the Greek New Testament, *heresy* usually means "faction" or "division."[33]

3. In later church usage, *heresy* referred to a denial of a defined doctrine of the Christian faith.[34]

    a. Bowman defines heresy as "a teaching which directly opposes the essentials of the Christian faith, so that true Christians must divide themselves from those who hold it."[35]

    b. To qualify as heresy, it must entail error on a central point of the Christian faith.[36]

    c. Thus, cultists are also heretics.

4. "Heretical" is the adjectival form of the word *heresy* (e.g., "a heretical teaching"), while a "heretic" is one who espouses heresy.

D. Sect

1. The word *sect* comes from the Latin *secta*, which means a "faction," "school of thought," or "political party."

2. The *American Heritage Dictionary* defines a sect as "a religious body, esp. one that has separated from a larger denomination."[37]

3. "Within the Christian tradition, the sect constitutes a distinctive, persisting and separately organized group of believers who reject the established religious authorities, but who claim to adhere to the authentic elements of the faith."[38]

4. Thus, the term "sect" can refer to genuinely Christian groups that "have distanced themselves from churches, and to some degree the predominant culture they represent, in order to emphasize one or more beliefs or practices they feel have been lost."[39]

---

[33]E.g., Acts 24:14 (which the NIV translates *sect*); 1 Corinthians 11:19; Galatians 5:19-20. See Robert M. Bowman, Jr., *Orthodoxy and Heresy: A Biblical Guide to Doctrinal Discernment* (Grand Rapids: Baker, 1992), 49.

[34]*Oxford Dictionary of the Christian Church*, ed. F. L. Cross and E. A. Livingstone (Oxford: Oxford Univ. Press, 1985), s.v. "Heresy," 639. Second Peter 2:1 also uses the word in this general sense.

[35]Bowman, *Orthodoxy and Heresy*, 50.

[36]John McClintock and James Strong, *Cyclopedia of Biblical, Theological, and Ecclesiastical Literature* (1867-1887; reprint, Grand Rapids: Baker, 1981), s.v. "Heresy," 4:199.

[37]*American Heritage Dictionary*, Second College Edition (Boston: Houghton Mifflin, 1985), 1108.

[38]Bryan Wilson, "Sect," in *The Westminster Dictionary of Christian Theology*, ed. Alan Richardson and John Bowden (Philadelphia: Westminster, 1983), 532. See also the discussion in Melton, *Encyclopedic Handbook of Cults in America*, 3.

[39]Samples et al., *Prophets of the Apocalypse*, 158-59.

Part II:
Statistics on Cults

I. The Difficulty in Determining Accurate Statistics

A. *Deciding Which Groups to Include*

1. Numbers given for total cult involvement range anywhere from 30,000[40] to 30 million.[41]

2. One of the main reasons for this wide disparity is disagreement over the definition of a cult.

    a. Some cult researchers—particularly those who base their definition on sociological criteria—have a broad and elastic definition.

    b. A definition that is too broad inflates the numbers.

        (1) Campus Crusade for Christ, charismatic Catholics, and Jews for Jesus have been lumped together with the cults, greatly inflating the number of "cult" members.[42]

        (2) As Bromley and Shupe caution, "The definitions of precisely what constituted a 'cult' or 'pseudo-religion' ran the gamut of personal preference and idiosyncratic prejudice for and against religious orthodoxy and theology, style of worship, belief origin, and virtually every other dimension of religious experience."[43]

    c. A definition that is too narrow will lead one to underestimate the numbers.

        (1) Some researchers do not consider Mormonism a cult because it is sociologically mainstream.

        (2) The Mormon church has roughly 9 million members worldwide; excluding a group of this size from the tally greatly affects the statistics.

---

[40]Anson D. Shupe, Jr. and David G. Bromley, *The New Vigilantes: Deprogrammers, Anti-Cultists, and the New Religions*, Sage Library of Social Research 113 (Beverly Hills and London: Sage Publications, 1980), 113-14.

[41]Walter R. Martin, *Martin Speaks Out on the Cults* (Ventura, Calif.: Vision House, 1983), 15. Paul Martin cites the same statistics; see Paul R. Martin, "Counseling the Former Cultist," in *Contend for the Faith: Collected Papers of the Rockford Conference on Discernment and Evangelism*, ed. Eric Pement (Chicago: Evangelical Ministries to New Religions, 1992), 262. In his classic *Kingdom of the Cults* Walter Martin placed the number at over 20 million (p. 16). In Martin's *Cults Reference Bible* (Part 3, p. 1) he estimated 24 million (Walter R. Martin, *The Cults Reference Bible* [Santa Ana, Calif.: Vision House, 1981]).

[42]William M. Alnor and Ronald Enroth, "Ethical Problems in Exit Counseling," *Christian Research Journal* (Winter 1992): 18; Tucker, *Another Gospel*, 16-17; Enroth, "What Is a Cult?" 10-11.

[43]Shupe and Bromley, *The New Vigilantes*, 113-14.

B. The Problem of Hysteria and Media Hype

"For a counter movement [i.e., the anti-cult movement] seeking to persuade the general public and officials of a pervasive, widespread, imminent threat to all persons, impressive statistics, however unsubstantiated, became important. At the 1979 'Dole hearing' in Washington, D.C., for example, anti-cult spokespersons variously claimed two million 'cult victims' and four million injured parents (AFF, 1979a:79) and ten million 'victims' (AFF, 1979a:25), while elsewhere deprogrammer Ted Patrick freely estimated twenty million Americans involved in cults (Siegelman and Conway, 1979:56)."[44]

C. The Approach Taken in This Book

1. The statistics given here reflect the definition of a cult given in Part I, section II.A; that is, we shall consider groups that claim to be Christian which at the same time deny one or more central doctrines of the Christian faith.

2. Since it is impossible to provide a number for total cult involvement—even according to the definition used in this book—I shall profile a few of the larger cults for which accurate statistics are available.

II. Statistical Estimates for "Cults"

A. General Statistics on Cultic Involvement

1. It is difficult to give a total number of cultists in the world or even in the U.S. (see section I above).

2. If one considers only Mormons and Jehovah's Witnesses, the two largest cults that fit the definition used in this book, the number of cultists totals nearly 14 million.

3. Adding in some of the other smaller yet significant cults, the number is at least 16 million.[45]

4. This 16 million figure is a conservative number because it only accounts for the major cult groups and does not take into account the many groups with small followings.

B. Mormonism

1. Membership Figures

   a. In 1991 there were approximately 8,120,000 Mormons worldwide.[46] The figure is now just under 9,000,000.

---

[44]Ibid., 120.

[45]Included in this approximate number is the Reorganized LDS Church (240,000); Christian Science (250,000), the Unification Church (2 million), and Unitarian Universalists (200,000). Concerning the Reorganized LDS Church, Kurt Van Gorden notes, "This is the largest existing splinter group.... It began in 1860 under the direction of Joseph Smith's eldest son, Joseph Smith III." For more information see the Mormonism volume in this series.

[46]*Church News* (11 April 1992): 4. Figures are for the year 1991.

     b. Mormons have more than 20,000 churches in 146 countries.[47]

     c. In 1992 there were 77,380 Children of Record Baptized.[48]

     d. In 1992 there were 274,477 conversions to Mormonism (down from 330,877 in 1990, but still strong compared to previous years).[49]

  2. Growth Rate

     a. *"Mormon membership on the average has doubled every 15 years since World War II, but from 1970 to 1985, it nearly tripled in size."*[50]

     b. "New Mormons are baptized at a rate of one every 1 minute 55 seconds."[51]

     c. "They are growing so rapidly that the *Mormon Church Almanac* proudly touts a third of a million baptisms annually, of which three quarters of those baptized were formerly Protestant."[52]

     d. Latin America is the place of most impressive Mormon growth.

     e. The Mormons project that they will have 12 to 14 million members by the year 2000.[53]

  3. Missionary Activity[54]

     a. Mormon teenagers are strongly encouraged to spend two years in missionary service, for which they raise their own support.[55]

     b. "Mormons field more than 46,000 full-time missionaries on two-year missions, up nearly 3,000 from the previous two years, spending more than one half billion dollars on missions work annually."[56]

     c. Note that of the third of a million baptisms annually, three quarters of those baptized were formerly Protestant.[57]

---

[47]Christian Research Institute, "Cult Growth Statistics" (September 1993), citing *The Ensign* (May 1993): 22.

[48]"Children of Record Baptized" refers to children born into Mormon families, age eight years and up. Mormons baptize children at the age of eight. Before that age children are considered incapable of committing sin.

[49]*Church News* (10 April 1993): 23.

[50]John Heinerman and Anson Shupe, *The Mormon Corporate Empire* (Boston: Beacon Press, 1985), 81.

[51]Christian Research Institute, "Cult Growth Statistics," citing *The Ensign* (May 1993): 22. This figure is based on the abovementioned 274,000 conversions for the year.

[52]Josh McDowell and Don Stewart, assisted by Kurt Van Gorden, *The Deceivers: What Cults Believe, How They Lure Followers* (San Bernardino, Calif.: Here's Life Publishers, 1992), 16.

[53]Heinerman and Shupe, *The Mormon Corporate Empire*, 81.

[54]See the Mormon publication by Julie A. Dockstader, "Media: Powerful Tool in Conversions," *Church News* (4 May 1991): 7.

[55]In many instances the missionary's family provides most, if not all, of the support. This support is in addition to the normal tithes given to the church.

[56]Christian Research Institute, "Cult Growth Statistics," citing *The Ensign* (May 1993): 22; LDS Church Statistical Info. Office (31 August 1993); *The Arizona Republic* (30 June-3 July 1991). See also *Church News* (10 April 1993): 23.

[57]McDowell and Stewart, *The Deceivers*, 16.

4. Literature Distribution and Media
   a. 679,815 people in the U.S. and Canada responded to Mormon media advertisements in 1990; of those, 198,091 agreed to have missionaries visit them.
   b. Mormons have also run TV ads with a toll-free number for obtaining copies of the Book of Mormon.[58]
   c. The Book of Mormon, or at least selections from it, is available in 79 languages.[59]
   d. Members donated 3.27 million copies of the Book of Mormon in 1990.

   According to the Mormon publication *Church News,* "Missionaries are very dependent on donated copies of the Book of Mormon. . . . Conversions to Christ through the Book of Mormon is the keystone of missionary work."[60]

5. Financial Holdings[61]
   a. Spring 1959 was the last time an official detailed financial report was made public.
   b. "The LDS church takes in $4.7 billion a year in income plus more than $3 billion annually in subsidiary business income—for a total that would rank it far wealthier than many nations of the world or such megacorporations as Union Carbide or Borden."[62]
   c. "The LDS church controls a $300 million-a-year media conglomerate, Bonneville International (some estimates run from $500 million to $1 billion), which reaches more than 2.3 million adults per year over Mormon-owned radio and television stations."[63]
   d. Members' tithes are an important source of Mormon income.
      (1) One-third of Mormons tithe regularly.[64]
      (2) The Mormon Church brings in about $3 million daily in tithes.
   e. The Mormons are second only to the Roman Catholic Church in total church wealth.[65]

---

[58]Dockstader, "Media: Powerful Tool in Conversions," 7.

[59]*The Ensign* (April 1991): 75.

[60]*Church News* (29 December 1990): 3.

[61]An important source for these figures is Heinerman and Shupe, the *Mormon Corporate Empire*. The authors provide a chart detailing Mormon corporate holdings (p. 80).

[62]Christian Research Institute, "Cult Growth Statistics," citing the *Arizona Republic* (30 June-3 July 1991).

[63]Ibid. The sources for these statistics are: Anson Shupe, *The Darker Side of Virtue: Corruption, Scandal and the Mormon Empire* (Buffalo: Prometheus Books, 1991), 29; Heinerman and Shupe, *The Mormon Corporate Empire*, n.p.; and *The Arizona Republic* (30 June-3 July 1991).

[64]Heinerman and Shupe, *The Mormon Corporate Empire*, 81.

[65]See Kurt Van Gorden's book on Mormonism in this series.

C. Jehovah's Witnesses

1. Membership Figures
   a. In 1993 there were 4,709,889 Jehovah's Witness "publishers" (i.e., active members) in 231 countries.
   b. 11,865,765 people attended the 1993 "Memorial" service (the Jehovah's Witness version of the Lord's Supper), which indicates that the general influence of the Witnesses is more than double the number of active members.[66]
   c. The Witnesses baptized 296,004 converts, or one baptized convert every 1 minute and 45 seconds.
   d. There are 73,070 congregations worldwide.
2. Growth Rate
   a. In 1993 the Jehovah's Witnesses grew 4.5 percent over 1992.
   b. "Nearly 27,000 new JWs were baptized in the former Soviet Union (Commonwealth of Independent States, Baltics, and other republics) last year, more than *tripling* the previous year's total; more than 66,000 JWs go door-to-door in the CIS."[67]
   c. Approximately 50 new Jehovah's Witness congregations form each week worldwide.[68]
3. Missionary Activity
   a. Jehovah's Witness publishers spent over one billion hours witnessing in 1993.[69]
   b. This works out to over 200 hours per Witness per year.
   c. They conducted 4,515,587 Bible studies each month with prospective converts.[70]
4. Literature Distribution and Media[71]
   a. The Jehovah's Witnesses make more extensive use of the printed word than any other cult.
   b. "The Watchtower Society operates 33 printing plants in countries around the world.....the main 'Bethel' plant in Brooklyn prints on almost 1,000 miles of paper or 61 million pages *per day* and turns out more than 3 million JW Bibles per month."[72]

---

[66]"1993 Service Year Report of Jehovah's Witnesses Worldwide," *The Watchtower* (1 January 1994): 13-15.

[67]Christian Research Institute, "Cult Growth Statistics," citing *The Watchtower* (1 January 1993): 15, 26.

[68]Ibid., citing the Watchtower Society video, *Jehovah's Witnesses: The Organization Behind the Name* (1990).

[69]"1993 Service Year Report of Jehovah's Witnesses Worldwide," 13-15.

[70]Ibid.

[71]An important book which discusses Watchtower literature, including its development historically, is David A. Reed, *Jehovah's Witness Literature: A Critical Guide to Watchtower Publications* (Grand Rapids: Baker, 1993).

[72]Christian Research Institute, "Cult Growth Statistics," citing *The Watchtower* (1 January 1993): 19b; Watchtower Society video, *Jehovah's Witnesses: The Organization Behind the Name* (1990).

c. "At some point during the late 1980s Jehovah's Witnesses published their 10-billionth (10,000,000,000th) piece of literature. It took more than one hundred years to produce all those books, booklets, magazines, and tracts since the first *Watch Tower* magazine rolled off the press in the summer of 1879, but the next 10 billion pieces of literature may take little more than a decade, if the sect continues to grow at its present rate."[73]

d. In 1991 there were more than 11,000 full-time factory and office workers running Watchtower operations (up from 5,000 in 1980).[74]

e. The Watchtower has translated their literature into 210 languages.[75]

f. *The Watchtower* magazine is one of their most significant publications.

(1) The *Watchtower* magazine has a twice-monthly printing exceeding 16 million copies per issue.

(2) It is available in 112 languages.

(3) Over 15 million copies per month are printed in English.[76]

(4) The magazine's circulation now rivals *Reader's Digest* and *TV Guide,* and outsells the combined total of *Time, Newsweek,* and *U.S. News & World Report.*[77]

g. "The JW's Bible (mis)translation, *New World Translation of the Holy Scriptures,* had seen 67 million copies printed in multiple languages as of 1990, having been rendered in whole or in part into 14 languages and is now being translated into 16 new European, African, and Asian languages."[78]

---

[73]Reed, *Jehovah's Witness Literature,* 9.

[74]Ibid., citing the *1991 Yearbook of Jehovah's Witnesses.*

[75]Christian Research Institute, "Cult Growth Statistics," citing Watchtower Society video, *Jehovah's Witnesses: The Organization Behind the Name* (1990).

[76]Ibid. See also *The Watchtower* (1 January 1993): 2.

[77]See Robert M. Bowman's book on Jehovah's Witnesses in this series.

[78]Christian Research Institute, "Cult Growth Statistics," citing *The Watchtower* (1 January 1993): 20a.

Part III: Theological Characteristics of Cults

I. Preliminary Considerations

A. *What do we mean by "theological characteristics of cults"?*

   1. The characteristics discussed in this section are *theological* because they describe how the group handles questions of religious doctrine.

   2. These characteristics have to do with the cultic *belief system* and the methods used in teaching and defending it.

   3. Theological characteristics are to be distinguished from the cult's behavioral (i.e., sociological) characteristics.

      a. The sociological characteristics of cults are treated later in the outline.[79]

      b. While a cult's theological beliefs relate directly to its practices, our focus here is on the characteristics of the belief system itself, not on the behavior that may follow from it.

B. *We must be careful not to apply these characteristics indiscriminately.*

   1. While the theological characteristics discussed in this section are commonly found in cults, this does not mean that all cults have all of them.

   2. These characteristics exist in varying degrees and in different combinations.

C. *Not all of these aberrant theological tendencies are equally serious.*

   1. Some of the characteristics given below relate to *core* beliefs (such as the cultic tendency to deny the Trinity and the deity of Christ), and such aberrations are exceedingly serious (see Part I, section II.B.6).

   2. Some theological characteristics of cults, while bad, do not automatically make the group cultic.

      For example, cults often emphasize experience over doctrine which, though unhealthy, does not make the group a cult.

D. *Some of these aberrant theological characteristics are found in genuinely Christian groups in varying degrees.*

   1. Certain charismatic Christian groups tend to emphasize experience over doctrine, but this does not make them cultic.

---

[79]See Part IV, section IV.

2. Christian denominations sometimes employ faulty principles of biblical interpretation, but unless the resulting interpretation involves a repudiation of core Christian beliefs, this characteristic does not make them cults.

    For example, certain genuinely Christian groups practice snake handling, based on a bizarre interpretation of Mark 16:18.

3. It is important to remember that what makes a group a cult is its denial of central Christian truths.

II. Common Theological Characteristics of Cults

A. Denial of the Trinity

1. Description

   a. The orthodox, biblical doctrine is that within the nature of the one God there are three eternal persons: the Father, Son, and Holy Spirit.[80]

   b. Probably all cults deny the doctrine of the Trinity.[81]

   c. Some deny the doctrine outright, usually labeling it "pagan."

   d. Other groups may claim to believe in the Trinity but redefine it so that the doctrine is not orthodox (e.g., teaching three gods instead of one God who exists in three persons).

2. Examples

   a. Jehovah's Witnesses

      (1) The Witnesses are known for their denial of the Trinity; they have been writing against the doctrine since the beginning.

      (2) The Witnesses consider the doctrine to be the result of pagan influences in the church.[82]

      (3) One of their recent works against the Trinity is entitled *Should You Believe in the Trinity?*—of course, the answer throughout the book is no!

   b. Mormonism

      (1) Mormons speak of the "Holy Trinity"[83] but redefine the doctrine into tritheism (i.e., three gods).

      (2) James Talmage, one of the Twelve Apostles of the Mormon church, states, "Father, Son, and Holy Ghost are as distinct in

---

[80]For a good introductory treatment of the doctrine of the Trinity, see E. Calvin Beisner, *God in Three Persons* (Wheaton, Ill.: Tyndale House, 1984).

[81]I say "probably" because it is possible (though inconsistent) for a group to affirm the Trinity but to deny some other central doctrine (e.g., the bodily resurrection). Though theoretically possible for a cult to affirm the Trinity, I am not aware of one that actually does.

[82]*Should You Believe in the Trinity?* (New York: Watchtower Bible and Tract Society, 1989), 8-12.

[83]E.g., James Talmage, *A Study of the Articles of Faith* (Salt Lake City: The Church of Jesus Christ of Latter-day Saints, 1976), Article 1, "God and the Holy Trinity," 29-51.

their persons and individualities as are any three personages in mortality."[84]

(3) The oneness that exists between the three "personages" in the Godhead is a oneness of purpose and agreement only.[85]

  c. William Branham

    (1) William Branham taught a modalistic view of the Trinity, also known as "oneness" doctrine.

    According to this teaching, Jesus and the Father are the same person; Jesus *is* the Father, appearing under a different mode of manifestation. Thus, modalists teach that Jesus is God, but as such he is the same person as the Father.

    (2) Branham states, "If Jesus is 'BOTH' Lord and Christ, then He (Jesus) is, and cannot be else but 'Father, Son, and Holy Ghost' in ONE Person manifested in the flesh. It is *NOT* 'God in three persons, blessed trinity,' but ONE GOD, ONE PERSON with three major titles, with three offices manifesting those titles."[86]

  d. United Pentecostal Church

    The United Pentecostal Church is another "oneness" cult, teaching a modalistic view of the Trinity.[87]

  e. Christian Science

    (1) Mary Baker Eddy denied the true deity of Christ and hence the Trinity.

    (2) Eddy stated, "Jesus Christ is not God, as Jesus himself declared, but is the Son of God."[88]

B. Denial of Salvation by Grace Through Faith

  1. Description

    a. Van Baalen urges us to remember that every cult ultimately teaches that we must save ourselves.[89]

    b. Though some cults pay lip service to the grace of God, they usually wind up teaching a kind of "works salvation" system.

      (1) Cultic works salvation is tied to their devaluation of Christ's work on the cross.[90]

---

[84]Ibid., Article 1, p. 41.

[85]Ibid.

[86]William Marrion Branham, *An Exposition of the Seven Church Ages* (Jeffersonville, Ind.: Spoken Word Publications, n.d.), 29. Emphasis in the original.

[87]A recent book which refutes the United Pentecostal view is Gregory A. Boyd, *Oneness Pentecostals and the Trinity* (Grand Rapids: Baker, 1992). See also E. Calvin Beisner's book in this series against modalistic cults.

[88]Mary Baker Eddy, *Science and Health with Key to the Scriptures* (Boston: Trustees Under the Will of Mary Baker G. Eddy, 1934), 361.

[89]J. K. Van Baalen, *The Chaos of the Cults* (Grand Rapids: Eerdmans, 1962), 359. Paul Martin makes the same observation in "Counseling the Former Cultist," 265.

[90]See discussion at point C below.

       (2) If Christ's work is not able to save fully then it must be supplemented in some way. The cults try to supplement the work of Christ through works of their own.

  2. Examples

    a. Mormonism

       (1) James Talmage called the doctrine of justification by faith alone "a most pernicious doctrine....Yet in spite of the plain word of God, dogmas of men have been promulgated to the effect that by faith alone may salvation be attained."[91]

       (2) In Mormon teaching, one is saved by "obedience to the laws and ordinances of the Gospel," which include faith, repentance, baptism by immersion for the remission of sins, and laying on of hands for the gift of the Holy Spirit.[92]

    b. Herbert W. Armstrong

       (1) Armstrong strongly denied that salvation comes solely from faith in Christ.

       (2) Armstrong stated, "[Satan] tries to deceive you into thinking all there is to it is just 'accepting Christ' with 'no works' and presto-chango, you are pronounced 'Saved.' But the *Bible* reveals that *none* is yet 'saved.'"[93]

       (3) Armstrong also said, "Just *believe* that's all there is to it; believe on the Lord Jesus Christ, and you are that instant *saved*! That teaching is false."[94]

    c. Swedenborgianism

      Emanuel Swedenborg, founder of the Church of New Jerusalem, stated, "They who place salvation in faith alone, when they read the Word, attend not at all to the things which are said therein concerning love and charity."[95]

C. Devaluation of the Work of Christ

  1. Description

    a. The cults often devalue Christ's atoning work on the cross, placing significant limitations on his saving work.

    b. Some say that Christ's atoning work only covers certain sins and not others.

---

[91]Talmage, *A Study of the Articles of Faith*, Article 4, pp. 107-8.

[92]See *Articles of Faith*, Articles 3 and 4.

[93]Herbert W. Armstrong, *Why Were You Born?* (Pasadena, Calif.: Ambassador Press, n.d.), 11.

[94]Herbert W. Armstrong, *All About Water Baptism* (Pasadena, Calif.: Ambassador Press, n.d.), 6.

[95]Emanuel Swedenborg, *Arcana Coelestina*, cited in *A Compendium of the Theological Writings of Emanuel Swedenborg*, comp. Samuel M. Warren (1875; reprint, New York: Swedenborg Foundation, 1974), 225.

        (1) For example, it might cover one's sins committed before joining the cult, but not those committed afterward.

        (2) Christ's work may have atoned for the sins of people who lived before his crucifixion but not for those who came after that time.

        (3) Christ's atonement may cover less serious sins but it cannot provide forgiveness for the more serious ones.

  c. Other groups teach that Christ was unable to complete his mission to redeem humankind completely; the cult must complete the work which Christ only began.

  d. Adding works as a condition of salvation devalues Christ's work because it implies that it is deficient.

2. Examples

  a. David Koresh

        (1) David Koresh taught that Christ's atonement only covered the sins of those who lived up to A.D. 31.

        (2) Koresh declared that he himself would have to die for the sins of those who lived from the New Testament era to the present.[96]

  b. Sun Myung Moon

        (1) Moon claims that Jesus failed to accomplish his mission, which was to provide physical and spiritual salvation.[97]

        (2) When it became obvious to Jesus that he would not be able to accomplish both, he settled for second best, which was to accomplish only spiritual salvation.[98]

        (3) Moon claims that the Lord of the Second Advent (presumably Moon) will provide physical salvation, thus completing the work that Jesus had hoped to accomplish the first time.

  c. Brigham Young

        (1) Brigham Young taught a doctrine known as "blood atonement," which is the teaching that sins too serious to be covered by the blood of Christ must be atoned for by the sinners themselves.

        (2) Young stated, "It is true that the blood of the Son of God was shed for sins ... yet men can commit sins which it can never remit."[99] "There is not a man or woman, who violates the covenants made with their God, that will not be required to pay

---

[96]Samples et al., *Prophets of the Apocalypse*, 205.

[97]Sun Myung Moon, *Divine Principle* (Washington, D.C.: The Holy Spirit Association for the Unification of World Christianity), 147.

[98]Ibid., 152.

[99]Journal of Discourses 4:54.

the debt. The blood of Christ will never wipe that out, your own blood must atone for it."[100]

(3) Thus, according to Mormon doctrine, we are able to atone for sins that even Jesus could not cover.

D. Denial of the Bodily Resurrection

1. Description
   a. The bodily resurrection of Christ is one of the central doctrines of the Christian faith (1 Cor. 15).
   b. Cults are well known for distorting the biblical teaching on the resurrection.
   c. The most common distortion is to spiritualize the resurrection. Rather than teaching that Christ rose from the dead in a physical body (Luke 24:39; John 2:19–21), some cults say that he rose in an ethereal spirit body.

2. Examples
   a. Jehovah's Witnesses
      (1) The Jehovah's Witnesses are well known for their denial of the bodily resurrection.
      (2) Joseph Franklin Rutherford stated, "The King Christ Jesus was put to death in the flesh and was resurrected an invisible spirit creature."[101]
   b. Herbert W. Armstrong
      (1) Speaking of Christ's resurrected body, Armstrong stated, "Nowhere does the Scripture say He was alive and active, or that God had Him get back into the human BODY that had died and was now resurrected.... And the resurrected body was no longer human ... it was the Christ resurrected, IMMORTAL, once *again* CHANGED!"[102]
      (2) Concerning the resurrection of humanity Armstrong stated, "The saints of God now born of the spirit and become spirit at the resurrection will be able to be invisible or visible at will."[103]

E. Reduction of the Absolute Authority of Scripture

1. Description
   a. Some cults expressly accuse the Bible of containing errors.
   b. Others undermine the authoritative revelation of Scripture by calling it "old light" which is subordinate to the "new light" of the cult.

---

[100] Journal of Discourses 3:247.

[101] Joseph Rutherford, *Let God Be True* (New York: Watchtower Bible and Tract Society, 1952), 122.

[102] Herbert W. Armstrong, "Why Christ Died and *Rose* Again!" *The Plain Truth* (April 1963): 10.

[103] Armstrong, *The Plain Truth* (October 1959): 30.

     c. A few cults have produced their own versions of the Bible, in which they mistranslate the Scriptures to support their doctrines.

     d. Certain cults undermine the authority of Scripture by adding extra sacred writings. These writings are typically given greater authority than the Bible.[104]

2. Examples

     a. People's Temple

"[Jim Jones] proceeded to systematically pick apart the Bible, a practice continued all the way to the end. Ex-members recall him going into tirades about the Bible, yelling and screaming that it was full of lies, tearing out pages, spitting on it, and stomping on it."[105]

     b. Mormonism

       (1) Joseph Smith's version of the Bible significantly alters the text to conform to Mormon teaching.

For example, the Joseph Smith version of Genesis 50 adds fourteen verses which "prophesy" the personal coming of Joseph Smith.

       (2) Mormons also undermine the authority of the Bible by questioning its accuracy.

The Mormon *Articles of Faith* says, "We believe the Bible to be the word of God as far as it is translated correctly; we also believe the Book of Mormon to be the word of God."[106] As Walter Martin has pointed out, in practical life this means that "wherever the Bible contradicts the Book of Mormon, the Bible is incorrectly translated." Note that Mormons place no such restriction on their own sacred books; the Book of Mormon is the word of God without qualification.

       (3) Mormons add the Book of Mormon, Doctrine and Covenants, and the Pearl of Great Price to the canon of Scripture, thus undermining the sufficiency of Scripture.

     c. Unification Church

Moon says, "It may be displeasing to religious believers, especially to Christians, to learn that a new expression of truth must appear.... The Bible, however, is not the truth itself, but a textbook teaching the truth."[107]

---

[104]Lewis, *Confronting the Cults*, 4.

[105]Sparks, *The Mindbenders*, 268. Jones's hostility to the Bible explodes the myth promulgated in the media that he was a "Christian fundamentalist." Ironically, Jones was actually *Marxist* in ideology—a philosophy arguably closer to that of the politically liberal media than to Christian fundamentalism (see pp. 259-60).

[106]*Articles of Faith*, Article 8.

[107]Moon, *Divine Principle*, 9.

F. Redefinition of Biblical Terminology

1. Description

   a. The cults typically use Christian vocabulary but radically redefine the terms.

      (1) As 2 Corinthians 11:4 states, there is another Jesus, a different spirit, and a different gospel from what the apostles preached (cf. Gal. 1:6–9).

      (2) Though the cults talk a great deal about Jesus, the gospel, salvation, etc., these are counterfeits of the biblical versions.

   b. This term switching is especially frustrating for a Christian trying to witness to a cultist.

      (1) Often the cultist will seem to agree with everything the Christian is saying about God, salvation, and Christ, but the agreement is illusory, because the cultist redefines biblical terminology in a sense foreign to its biblical usage.

      (2) As Walter Martin pointed out, "Many fruitless hours of discussion with cultists [get] the Christian nowhere because of failing to define terms."[108]

      (3) For a Christian to be effective in witnessing to the cultist, he or she should be familiar with how the cult defines key terms in the particular cultic system.[109]

2. Examples

   a. Unity School of Christianity

      (1) Martin cites the "mind science" cults as good examples of groups that redefine biblical terms.[110]

      (2) The *Metaphysical Bible Dictionary,* published by Unity School of Christianity, is "the masterpiece of redefinition."[111]

      For example, the *Metaphysical Bible Dictionary* defines heaven and hell as "states of mind, and conditions, which people experience as a direct outworking of their thoughts, beliefs, words, and acts."[112] Christ is "the divine-idea man.... This Christ, or perfect-man idea existing eternally in Divine Mind, is the true, spiritual, higher self of every individual. Each of us has within him the Christ, just as Jesus had."[113] Adam was "the first movement of mind in its contact with life and substance."[114]

---

[108]Martin, *Kingdom of the Cults,* 19.

[109]Ibid., 24.

[110]Ibid., 20.

[111]Ibid., 21. The Unity School of Christianity is covered by Todd Ehrenborg in the mind sciences volume in this series.

[112]*Metaphysical Bible Dictionary* (Kansas City: Unity School of Christianity, 1942), s.v. "Hell," 271.

[113]Ibid., s.v. "Christ," 150.

[114]Ibid., s.v. "Adam," 23.

b. Mormonism

(1) According to Mormonism, God is an exalted man.

Joseph Smith taught that "God himself was once as we are now, and is an exalted Man."[115]

(2) Indeed, the Mormons contend that the "sectarian" view, which denies that God has a physical body, is actually a denial of God.[116] In reality, the "sectarian" (i.e., true Christian) view is the clear teaching of Scripture (Num. 28:19; John 4:24).

(3) Thus, when Mormons speak of their "Heavenly Father," Christians should not assume they are using the term in the same way the Bible uses it. The biblical God is not a man (Num. 23:19)—exalted or otherwise.

G. *Exclusivistic Belief System*

1. Description

a. Cults often claim to have the sole corner on the truth.[117]

(1) Sometimes the cultic belief system is mediated through an "inspired" leader, who is considered to be God's modern-day mouthpiece.[118]

(2) In other groups the emphasis is placed on the organization as God's sole channel of revelation.

b. Cultic exclusivism should not be confused with Christianity's exclusive teaching that faith in Jesus Christ is the only way of salvation.

(1) Jesus was exclusivistic when he said, "I am the way and the truth and the life. No one comes to the Father except through me" (John 14:6). But then, in making this exclusive claim Jesus was merely telling the truth.

(2) The apostles were exclusivistic when they taught that "salvation is found in no one else, for there is no other name under heaven given to men by which we must be saved" (Acts 4:12). Here again, the apostles were merely reiterating Christ's own teaching.

(3) Cultic exclusivism, in contrast, is wrongly directed and based on a lie.

In cultic exclusivism one must place faith in the teachings of the cult leader or the cultic organization, even though the cult's teachings contradict the words of Jesus Christ.

c. Some secular anti-cultists, such as Conway and Siegelman, see no real difference between Christian and cultic exclusivity, and con-

---

[115]Joseph Smith, Journal of Discourses 6:3.

[116]Talmage, *A Study of the Articles of Faith*, Article 1, p. 48.

[117]See Martin, *Kingdom of the Cults*, 26.

[118]Sparks, *The Mindbenders*, 24.

sequently they sometimes wrongly compare genuinely evangelical Christian groups with cults.[119]

2. Examples

   a. Jehovah's Witnesses

      (1) The Watchtower Bible and Tract Society says that it is the one true religious organization. Specifically, the hierarchy of the Watchtower Bible and Tract Society is "the faithful and wise servant," which "dispenses (doctrinal) food in due season."[120]

      (2) All true Christians must submit to this teaching.

   b. Mormonism

      James Talmage stated: "Latter-day Saints ... boldly proclaim the conviction that their Church is the accepted one, the only one entitled to the designation 'Church of Jesus Christ' and the sole earthly repository of the eternal Priesthood in the present age.... My allegiance to the Church of my choice is based on a conviction of the validity and genuineness of its high claim—as the one and only Church possessing a God-given charter of authority."[121]

H. Compartmentalization of Conflicting Facts

1. Description

Dr. Walter Martin describes how some cults "compartmentalize" conflicting facts.[122] Compartmentalization is a process in which cults selectively ignore facts that obviously contradict their claims.

2. Examples

   a. Jehovah's Witnesses

      (1) The Jehovah's Witnesses have made many prophesies that did not come true, and yet they do not abandon their system of prophetic interpretation or the Watchtower Society.

      (2) For example, the Witnesses predicted that Armageddon would occur in 1914, 1915, 1918, and 1975. Even though the end did not come, Witnesses continue to assert that the Watchtower Society is the only organization that speaks God's prophetic truth.[123]

---

[119]Conway and Siegelman, *Snapping*, 45-46.

[120]For a discussion of the Watchtower view of authority see their publications *You Can Live Forever in Paradise on Earth* (1982), 191-95; and *Reasoning from the Scriptures* (1985), 281-83. Robert Bowman discusses this subject in the volume on Jehovah's Witnesses in this series.

[121]James Talmage, *A Study of the Articles of Faith*, Article 11, p. 403.

[122]Martin, *Kingdom of the Cults*, 28-29.

[123]*The Watchtower* (1 April 1972). Some Jehovah's Witnesses have left the organization because of these failed prophecies, but the vast majority continue in the organization despite such obviously false predictions.

    b. Mormonism

       (1) Mormons have changed the Book of Mormon over 3,913 times to correct its errors,[124] and yet they maintain that the Book of Mormon was given by direct inspiration from God and is the "most perfect book on earth."[125]

       (2) The manuscript for the Book of Abraham, a work that is part of the Pearl of Great Price, was discovered and was translated by professional Egyptologists. With the actual text in hand, it was possible to verify independently the accuracy of Joseph Smith's "inspired translation." The Egyptologists discovered that the actual translation of the text had nothing in common with Joseph Smith's translation.[126] Yet, the Mormons continue to regard the Book of Abraham as inspired literature.[127]

    c. Christian Science

       (1) Mary Baker Eddy's personal history directly and blatantly contradicts the teachings of her cult.

       (2) Though she denied the reality of sickness, claiming that it is an illusion, Eddy herself was often sick and served by doctors. For example, she was injected with morphine for pain control, wore glasses, and had her teeth removed.

       (3) Nevertheless, Eddy's followers continue to hold to her teaching that sickness is an illusion.[128]

I. Rejection of the Doctrine of Eternal Punishment

  1. Description

Many cults reject the biblical doctrine of eternal punishment.

    a. Universalism

Some replace the biblical teaching about hell with universalism, which is the idea that all people eventually will be saved.

    b. Annihilationism[129]

Others deny the doctrine of hell by teaching annihilationism, which is the teaching that God will take the wicked out of existence.

---

[124]Martin, *Kingdom of the Cults*, 29. Two excellent sources by Jerald Tanner and Sandra Tanner that document these changes are *Mormonism: Shadow or Reality*, 4th ed. (Salt Lake City: Utah Lighthouse Ministry, 1982), and *The Changing World of Mormonism* (Chicago: Moody Press, 1980).

[125]Joseph Smith stated, "I told the brethren that the Book of Mormon was the most correct book of any book on the earth, and the keystone of our religion" (Joseph Smith, quoted in the introduction to the Book of Mormon, 1991 ed.).

[126]In reality, the papyrus of the so-called Book of Abraham is an Egyptian funerary text containing portions of the Egyptian "Book of the Dead."

[127]One of the best recent discussions of the Book of Abraham is Charles M. Larson, *By His Own Hand upon Papyrus: A New Look at the Joseph Smith Papyri* (Grand Rapids: Institute for Religious Research, 1985, 1992).

[128]Martin, *Kingdom of the Cults*, 29.

[129]There is an increasing number of evangelicals who espouse the annihilationist view. While the evangelicals who hold this view should not be regarded as cultists for doing so, it is nevertheless a grave and

Thus, the wicked do not suffer eternal torment but simply cease to exist.

2. Examples

    a. Jehovah's Witnesses

      (1) Throughout their nearly 115-year history, Jehovah's Witnesses have been some of the most strident critics of the doctrine of hell.

      (2) Joseph Franklin Rutherford, an early Watchtower leader, stated, "Who is responsible for this God-dishonoring doctrine? And what is his purpose? The promulgator of it is Satan himself; and his purpose in introducing it has been to frighten the people away from studying the Bible and to make them hate God."[130]

      (3) Jehovah's Witnesses maintain the same vigorous opposition to this day.[131]

    b. Herbert W. Armstrong

      (1) Like the Watchtower, Herbert W. Armstrong taught the eventual annihilation of the wicked.

      (2) Armstrong stated, "The wages of sin is death" (Romans 6:23) and the death, which is the absence of life, is for ALL ETERNITY. It is eternal punishment by remaining DEAD for all eternity—not remaining alive and being tortured in a fictitious, burning hell-fire!"[132]

    c. Unitarian Universalists

      (1) As their name implies, Unitarian Universalists not only deny the Trinity but also the doctrine of eternal punishment.

      (2) Instead, they teach universal salvation.[133]

J. *Emphasis on Experience over Doctrine*

1. Description

    a. Some cults give undue prominence to feelings and emotions at the expense of rational thought.

    b. It may be difficult to reach the experientially oriented cultist through rational argumentation; he or she may not care whether the cult's teachings are true, so long as they produce a good feeling.

    c. There is nothing wrong with feelings and experiences, when kept in their proper place.

---

inexcusable error. I have refuted the annihilationist position in a two-part article (Alan W. Gomes, "Evangelicals and the Annihilation of Hell," *Christian Research Journal* 13-14 [Spring 1991 and Summer 1991]).

[130]Rutherford, *Let God Be True*, 79.

[131]For recent discussions of the Jehovah's Witness position on the afterlife, including the doctrine of hell, see *You Can Live Forever in Paradise on Earth*, 76-89; and *Reasoning from the Scriptures*, 98-100, 168-75, 375-79, 382-83. Bowman discusses these texts in the Jehovah's Witnesses volume in this series.

[132]Herbert W. Armstrong, "*Immortality*," 7, cited in McDowell and Stewart, *The Deceivers*, 290. Emphasis in the original.

[133]Mather and Nichols, *Dictionary*, 286. See also my volume on the Unitarian Universalists in this series.

        (1) Scripture commands us to love the Lord our God with all of our heart, soul and mind (Deut. 6:5; Matt. 22:37; Mark 12:30; Luke 10:27), illustrating that worship involves both our emotions and our intellects.

        (2) For the Christian, however, true faith is founded on fact, not feeling.

        (3) Cultic faith is sometimes based on "a burning in the bosom" (e.g., Mormonism) rather than on truth.[134]

    d. Not all cults are experience oriented. For example, Jehovah's Witnesses tend to be much more rationalistic.[135]

  2. Examples

    a. Mormonism

        (1) Mormons will often speak of a "burning in the bosom"—a warm, emotional feeling that confirms to them that the Book of Mormon is true and that Joseph Smith is a prophet of God.

        (2) This experience is mentioned in Doctrine and Covenants 9:8–9: "Behold, I [God] say unto you, that you must study it out in your mind; then you must ask me if it be right, and if it is right I will cause that your bosom shall burn within you; therefore, you shall feel that it is right. But if it be not right you shall have no such feelings."[136]

        (3) Mormons also cite Luke 24:32 (KJV): "Did not our heart burn within us, while he talked with us by the way, and while he opened to us the scriptures?"

        (4) When Mormon missionaries confront opposition to the Book of Mormon during a witnessing encounter, they will often urge the prospective convert to "pray about it" to see if God will grant a "testimony of the Holy Ghost" (known among Mormons as a "burning in the bosom" experience), which will confirm the truth of Mormonism.

    b. Urantia[137]

        (1) Bill Sadler claims that the *Urantia Book* was dictated to him by seven spirit beings from another world.

        (2) In 1989 I moderated a discussion between Robert and Gretchen Passantino (two Christian apologists from Answers in Action) and a representative of the Urantia position.

---

[134]See point 2.a below.

[135]John Allan, *Shopping for a God: Fringe Religions Today* (Grand Rapids: Baker, 1986), 111-12; Martin, *Kingdom of the Cults*, 63-66.

[136]Note that Joseph Smith is speaking here of the translation work of the Book of Mormon. Mormons have applied this generally to discerning the truth of the Book of Mormon.

[137]Technically, Urantia is not a cult of Christianity since its adherents do not claim to be Christians. They often claim, however, that their beliefs are compatible with Christianity.

(3) When pressed to defend how he knew the *Urantia Book* was true, the Urantia representative finally admitted, "I believe it is true because it makes me feel good to believe it. Belief in this book has changed my life."

K. Emphasis on Direct Revelations and Visions from God

1. Description

   a. Certain cults, and particularly the leaders of these cults, maintain that God speaks directly to them.

   b. Such people have a direct line to God, which others do not possess.

   c. Sometimes the "revelations" deal with future events; other times the "words from the Lord" are directed to the contemporary circumstances of the group.

   d. Scripture tells us, "Test everything. Hold on to the good" (1 Thess. 5:21).

      (1) If a prediction does not come true, then we can be sure that the prophecy (and the prophet) is not from God.

      Biblical prophets never erred: "If what a prophet proclaims in the name of the LORD does not take place or come true, that is a message the LORD has not spoken. That prophet has spoken presumptuously" (Deut. 18:22).

      (2) If the prophecy contradicts what God has previously revealed in his word, then the prophecy is false.

      "To the law and to the testimony! If they do not speak according to this word, they have no light of dawn" (Isa. 8:20).

2. Examples

   a. Mormonism

      (1) Joseph Smith claimed to receive visions.

      For example, in the spring of 1820, Smith supposedly received a vision of God the Father and Jesus Christ. In this vision Smith was told not to join any of the Christian denominations, "for they were all wrong" and "all their creeds were an abomination."[138] On September 21, 1823, Joseph Smith declared that an angel named Moroni appeared to him, telling him of golden plates that contained what was to become the Book of Mormon. Moroni supposedly appeared again in 1827, giving Smith permission to dig up the plates and begin translation work. In May 1829, John the Baptist supposedly appeared to Smith and to Oliver Cowdery, conferring the Aaronic priesthood on them.[139]

---

[138]Pearl of Great Price (1851; rev. ed, Salt Lake City: Church of Jesus Christ of Latter-day Saints, 1981), 1:19.

[139]As Kurt Van Gorden notes, "Biblically, the Aaronic priesthood could only be held by a descendant of Levi (Exodus 4:14; 29:1), hence the Levitical priesthood. Its purpose was to offer sacrifices for Israel (Hebrews 5:1-3). There is no need for the Aaronic or Levitical priesthood after Jesus' crucifixion, since Jesus is the ultimate sacrifice for sins (Hebrews 7:27; 9:11-14)." See his book on Mormonism in this series.

(2) Brigham Young stated, "I have had many revelations; I have seen and heard for myself; and know these things are true, and nobody on earth can disprove them."[140]

(3) Mormon prophets and apostles have made predictions about future events that never happened.

McDowell and Stewart note that Joseph Smith gave "at least ten well-documented false prophesies."[141] For example, Joseph Smith uttered false prophecies concerning the Civil War, including the claim that Great Britain would become involved and would fight on the side of the North.[142] Smith also prophesied that war would be poured out on "all nations," which obviously did not happen. Also, in 1856 Herber C. Kimball, First Counselor to the President, prophesied that Brigham Young would become president of the United States.[143]

b. Unification Church

(1) Sun Myung Moon claims that Jesus Christ appeared to him on Easter morning of 1936.

(2) Jesus supposedly asked Moon to complete the work that he (Jesus) had begun almost 2000 years earlier.[144]

c. Swedenborgianism

Emanuel Swedenborg claimed to have received many visions of the spirit world, including visions of heaven and hell.

L. Claims of Miracles, Signs, and Wonders

1. Description

a. Some cults claim to be able to perform miracles, signs, and wonders. Naturally, it is impossible to test all such claims.

b. Any group that denies the essentials of the Christian faith cannot perform genuine miracles in the power of the true God.

c. Some cultic miracles might occur through the agency of Satan; this is what the Bible calls "counterfeit miracles, signs and wonders" (2 Thess. 2:9).

d. In other cases, cultic "miracles" are hoaxes and not miraculous at all.[145]

---

[140] Journal of Discourses 16:46.

[141] McDowell and Stewart, *The Deceivers*, 26-27.

[142] Doctrine and Covenants, 87.

[143] Journal of Discourses 5:219. See also Tanner, *Mormonism: Shadow or Reality?* 418.

[144] See J. Isamu Yamamoto, *The Puppet Master: An Inquiry into Sun Myung Moon and the Unification Church* (Downers Grove, Ill.: InterVarsity Press, 1977), 16. In addition, see the Unification Church volume in this series, also by Yamamoto.

[145] André Kole has exposed a number of such frauds in his *Miracles or Magic?* (Eugene, Ore.: Harvest House, 1987). See also André Kole and Terry Holley's book on astrology and psychics in this series.

2. Examples
   a. Christian Science
      (1) This group boasts that healings frequently have taken place as a result of Christian Science principles.
      (2) The Christian Science Church publishes and distributes a book entitled *A Century of Christian Science Healing*. This book is filled with testimonies of people who say that they have been healed through practicing Christian Science.[146]
   b. People's Temple
      (1) Jim Jones asserted that he raised more than 40 people from the dead.[147]
      (2) Jones even claimed to have raised *himself* from the dead.

      Jones faked his own assassination in the parking lot of his church, pretending to have been shot. All the members of the congregation were herded into the temple, supposedly for their protection. Suddenly Jones appeared, holding his bloodstained shirt with two holes in it. He declared that he had raised himself from the dead.[148] People associated with Jones later testified to the fraud.

      (3) Jones also said he was the reincarnation of Christ.

      After making this claim, Jones held up his hands, which appeared to be bleeding. A former aide stated, however, that the "blood" came from capsules hidden in his fists.[149]

M. Fixation with the End Times
1. Description
   a. Many cults are fixated with eschatology (eschatology is the study of the "end times," or "last things," including the second coming of Christ).
   b. Often associated with this fixation is the idea that only those who are members of the cult will be spared the impending doom.
   c. Cults fixated with eschatology sometimes have set dates for the end, usually based on bizarre interpretations of the biblical text (e.g., the Book of Revelation).
   d. Of course, there is a legitimate Christian interest in end times which is not cultic.
      (1) Simply because the cults are obsessed with eschatology does not mean that Christians should avoid the subject altogether.

---

[146]*A Century of Christian Science Healing* (Boston: Christian Science Publishing Society, 1966).

[147]Sparks, *The Mindbenders*, 264-65.

[148]Ibid., 269.

[149]Ibid., 269-70.

After all, the prophetic portions of the Bible are also the Word of God.

(2) Christians believe that a day of judgment *is* coming for those who reject Christ as their savior (Matt. 25:31–46; Heb. 9:27; Rev. 20:12–15).

(3) Belief in a day of judgment is not cultic but is the clear teaching of Scripture, which Christians through the centuries have professed (e.g., the Apostle's Creed).

e. Sometimes Christians have been irresponsible in handling biblical prophecy.

(1) For example, during the recent war in the Persian Gulf, some Christians read all manner of eschatological significance into the events (e.g., identifying Saddam Hussein as the Antichrist).

(2) Some, such as Edgar Whisenant, have written books confidently calculating the exact date of the rapture, the tribulation, and other end time events.[150]

Such prophecy mongering only makes Christians look foolish.

(3) Christians should take note of this cultic fixation with the end times before making confident eschatological predictions that go beyond the biblical evidence.

2. Examples

a. Jehovah's Witnesses

(1) The Jehovah's Witnesses have falsely predicted that Armageddon would occur in 1914, 1915, 1918, and 1975.

(2) They have made at least 14 false predictions of this sort.[151]

b. Branch Davidians[152]

(1) When Branch Davidian founder Victor Houteff died, his wife Florence took over as the prophetess for the group.

(2) Florence Houteff predicted that April 22, 1959, would mark the end of the 1,260 days of Revelation 11 and the beginning of the judgments of Ezekiel 9.

God was supposed to remove the Jews and Arabs from Palestine and usher in the Davidic kingdom. The second coming of Christ might also occur at this time.

(3) "In response to Florence's announcement more than 1,000 'true believers' sold all their possessions, gave their money to the church, and gathered at Mt. Carmel."[153]

---

[150]E.g., Whisenant's *88 Reasons Why the Rapture Will Be in 1988*, later revised to *The Final Shout: Rapture Report—1989*.

[151]McDowell and Stewart, *The Deceivers*, 26-27. Some of these false prophecies are listed on 102-4.

[152]Christian Research Institute International, "The Branch Davidians, Statement Number DD–025," prepared by Richard Abanes (11 March 1993), 2.

[153]Ibid.

(4) When nothing happened on April 22, many believers left the movement or became involved in one of the several factions that formed.

c. People's Temple

In 1965, Jim Jones predicted that Indianapolis would be destroyed in a thermonuclear war that would start on July 15, 1967.[154]

d. Children of God

Children of God leader Moses David said that the comet Kohoutek would destroy the U.S. in 1974.[155]

N. Denial of the Priesthood of the Believer

1. Description

a. The Bible teaches that *all* believers are priests (1 Peter 2:4–10; Rev. 1:6; 5:10), meaning all believers have direct access to God (Heb. 4:16).

b. Most cultic groups insist that in order for people to understand God's truth, they must submit to the teaching of the cult leader or organization, thus denying the priesthood of all believers (cf. 1 John 2:26–27).

2. Examples

a. Branch Davidians

David Koresh claimed to be the only one who could interpret Scripture for his followers.[156]

b. Jehovah's Witnesses

(1) Charles Taze Russell, founder of the Jehovah's Witnesses, claimed that his *Studies in the Scriptures* were "indispensable" for understanding the divine plan.

(2) Russell stated:

"Not only do we find that people cannot see the divine plan in studying the Bible by itself, but we see, also, that if anyone lays the 'Scripture Studies' aside, even after he has used them, after he has become familiar with them, after he has read them for ten years—if he then lays them aside and ignores them and goes to the Bible alone, though he has understood his Bible for ten years, our experience shows that within two years he goes into darkness."[157]

---

[154]Sparks, *The Mindbenders*, 263.

[155]Moses David, "40 Days and Nineveh Shall Be Destroyed." Tract published in 1973.

[156]Abanes, "The Branch Davidians," 4.

[157]Charles Taze Russell, quoted in Anthony A. Hoekema, *The Four Major Cults* (Grand Rapids: Eerdmans, 1963), 227.

(3) The Watchtower continues this belief today, maintaining that one must submit to the Watchtower organization to understand divine truth.[158]

c. Unification Church

(1) According to Moon, human history is divided into three dispensations: Moses revealed God's truth in the Old Testament age, Jesus revealed God's truth in the New Testament age, and Moon reveals God's truth in the Completed Testament age.

(2) The introduction to the *Divine Principle* states: "With the fullness of time, God has sent His messenger to resolve the fundamental questions of life and the universe. His name is Sun Myung Moon."[159]

O. Disregard for Sound Hermeneutical Principles

1. Description

a. Hermeneutics is the science of interpreting a document.

b. Cults employ unsound and even bizarre methods of interpretation to support their cultic doctrine.

c. This is often displayed in the cultists' failure to interpret Scripture in its context.

Walter Martin stated, "Let it never be forgotten that cultists are experts at lifting texts out of their respective contexts, without proper concern for the laws of language or the established principles of 'Biblical interpretation.'"[160]

d. Sometimes Christians are guilty of faulty biblical interpretation, though certainly not to the degree of the cults.

(1) Christians should be careful to practice sound methods of biblical interpretation.

(2) Some good standard works on biblical hermeneutics can be most beneficial.[161]

2. Examples

a. Jehovah's Witnesses

(1) The Jehovah's Witnesses rarely deal with what is stated before and after the verses they share. Often when the verses are interpreted within their context they not only fail to prove the Watchtower doctrine but prove just the opposite.

---

[158]The arguments for this position are discussed in Bowman's Jehovah's Witness volume in this series. Bowman cites *You Can Live Forever in Paradise on Earth* (1982), 191-95; and *Reasoning from the Scriptures* (1985), 281-83.

[159]Moon, *Divine Principle*, 16.

[160]Martin, *Kingdom of the Cults*, 23.

[161]For a discussion of the various genres of biblical literature and the principles that govern their interpretation see Gordon D. Fee and Douglas Stuart, *How to Read the Bible for All Its Worth*, 2d. ed. (Grand Rapids: Zondervan, 1993). For a more technical work on biblical interpretation see Grant R. Osborne, *The Hermeneutical Spiral: A Comprehensive Introduction to Biblical Interpretation* (Downers Grove, Ill.: Inter-Varsity Press, 1991).

(2) For example, the Watchtower uses Philippians 2 to teach against the deity of Christ, when verses 10–11 show that Jesus receives the same worship as Jehovah.

(3) Another example is Hebrews 1:1, which the Witnesses use to "prove" that Jesus was a created being.

Not only does this verse fail to prove their point, but a few verses later Jesus is described as "the exact representation" of God's nature—a statement that hardly fits the Watchtower's view of Christ.

   b. Christian Science

(1) Mary Baker Eddy said that if we are to understand the true significance of the name "Adam," we must do the following:

"Divide the name Adam into two syllables, and it reads, *a dam*, or obstruction. . . . it stands for obstruction, error, even the supposed separation of man from God."[162]

(2) This bizarre interpretation is refuted simply by noting that the English word "dam" and the Hebrew word "Adam" have nothing whatever in common, linguistically speaking.

P. Syncretism

1. Description

   a. Syncretism refers to the blending of different—and often contradictory—teachings into a kind of heretical stew.

   b. A syncretistic approach certainly does not apply to all cults and false religious systems, but some of them, especially those that depend on Eastern thought, do fall into this category.

2. Examples

   a. Unification Church

(1) Moon's theology draws on elements of Eastern religion.

(2) Braswell states, "The theology [of Moon] is rooted in Asian concepts including backgrounds in animism, shamanism, tribalism, Confucianism, and Buddhism. Christian concepts and biblical data are meshed together with Korean religious traditions in particular."[163]

(3) For example, Moon uses the concept of yin and yang to speak of the "dual essentialities" in God.[164]

   b. Herbert W. Armstrong

(1) Herbert Armstrong used an eclectic approach.[165]

---

[162]Eddy, *Science and Health*, 338.

[163]Braswell, *Understanding Sectarian Groups in America,* 109.

[164]Moon, *Divine Principle*, 27.

[165]Martin, *Kingdom of the Cults*, 305.

(2) Armstrong borrowed from the Seventh-day Adventists (the Sabbath and dietary laws), Jehovah's Witnesses (not observing Christian holidays) and Swedenborgianism (Anglo-Israelism).[166]

(3) Note, however, that in the process of borrowing, Armstrong makes his modifications to these doctrines, so the teachings bear his stamp.

Q. Involvement in Spiritism/the Occult

1. Description

   a. Occultic involvement does not characterize most or even many cults, but it is found in some (see Part I, section IV.B. above).

   b. For example, some cults and cult leaders engage in spirit contact.

2. Examples

   a. Children of God[167]

      (1) Moses David claimed to receive messages from Abrahim, a former Gypsy King of Bulgaria.

      (2) He also was "in contact" with Martin Luther, Ivan the Terrible, William Jennings Bryan, Peter the Hermit, Anne Boleyn, and a host of other famous historical personages.

   b. Unification Church

      (1) Moon stated, "There are many people on earth today who can communicate with the spirit world,"[168] regarding this as a fulfillment of Acts 2:17.

      (2) Some followers of Moon have visions of Moon and his wife during prayer and have contact with spirits.[169]

   c. Mormonism

      (1) Joseph Smith dabbled in occultic practices.[170]

      (2) For example, Smith made use of seer stones,[171] talismans,[172] and other occult paraphernalia.

---

[166]Anglo-Israelism is the teaching that the United States and Britain are to be identified as the ten lost tribes of Israel. Thus, statements about Israel in biblical prophecy are applied to the United States and Britain. Interestingly, the Worldwide Church appears to be on the verge of repudiating the Anglo-Israel doctrine; see Phillip Arnn, "Leaked WCG Memo Questions British Israelism," *Watchman Expositor* 10, no. 7 (1993): 5-6.

[167]Allan, *Shopping for a God*, 149. Moses David's deep involvement with the occult and spirit contact is well documented in *The New Cults*, 191-96.

[168]Moon, *Divine Principle*, 177.

[169]McDowell and Stewart, *The Deceivers*, 24-25.

[170]Joseph Smith's involvement with the occult is discussed in Kurt Van Gorden's book on Mormonism in this series.

[171]Seer stones were stones that functioned somewhat like crystal balls. The stones were placed in a hat and then by looking at these stones the occult practitioner would see visions in them. The actual seer stones used by Joseph Smith are pictured in D. Michael Quinn's *Early Mormonism and the Magic World View* (Salt Lake City: Signature Books, 1987).

[172]A talisman is an "object onto which is engraved a symbol or picture of a character that is believed to harness powers to protect or prosper the owner or possessor" (Mather and Nichols, *Dictionary*, s.v. "Talismans," 270).

R. Tendency to See Scripture as Alluding to Their Cultic Movement

1. Description

   a. Some cults claim that the Bible foretells the coming of their particular movement. Thus, they "read themselves into the Bible" in a very strange way.

   b. This is a specific instance of disregarding sound hermeneutical principles.[173]

2. Examples

   a. Jehovah's Witnesses

   The Jehovah's Witnesses claim that the faithful and wise servant mentioned in Luke 12:42 is a direct prophetic reference to the Watchtower hierarchy.

   b. Children of God

   The Children of God believe that verses in 1 John using the phrase "children of God" (1 John 3:10; 5:2) are speaking of their cult by name.

   c. Mormonism

   In the Joseph Smith Translation of the Bible, Smith added fourteen verses to Genesis chapter 50, so that the "future" coming of Joseph Smith would be "prophesied."

   d. Branch Davidians

   (1) David Koresh claimed that he was the "antitype" of King David in the Old Testament.[174]

   Koresh also claimed to be the antitypical Cyrus of Isaiah 45 (*Koresh* is Hebrew for "Cyrus"). Thus, everything Koresh did was regarded as led by God (based on the KJV rendering of Isa. 45:13).

   (2) Koresh also claimed to be the Lamb spoken of in Revelation 6.[175]

S. Emphasis on Minor Points of Theology[176]

1. Description

   a. Bernard Ramm notes that a cult often "places a secondary need in the position of a primary need."[177]

---

[173]See point O above.

[174]The word *type* comes from the Greek word meaning "form" or "pattern." "Typology deals with the principle of analogous fulfillment.... Biblical typology involves an analogical correspondence in which earlier events, persons, and places in salvation history become patterns by which later events and the like are interpreted." The "antitype" is the resulting "copy" of the type. Thus, Adam is a type of Christ (Rom. 5:14) and Christ is the antitype of Adam (Walter Elwell, ed., *Evangelical Dictionary of Theology* [Grand Rapids: Baker, 1984], s. v. "Type, Typology," by G. R. Osborne, 1117-18).

[175]Abanes, "The Branch Davidians," 4.

[176]Hoekema, *The Four Major Cults,* 375.

[177]Bernard Ramm, cited in Lewis, *Confronting the Cults,* 4.

b. Some cults make a big deal about dress, the day of worship, celebrating holidays and birthdays, saluting the flag, etc.

c. The Christian should try to steer the conversation to truly important issues, such as the person of Christ and his saving work.

2. Examples

a. Jehovah's Witnesses

Jehovah's Witnesses place great emphasis on not observing holidays and not saluting the flag.

b. Herbert W. Armstrong

(1) Armstrong stressed the importance of observing Old Testament dietary laws, keeping the Sabbath, women not wearing cosmetics, and avoiding doctors.

(2) Note that the Worldwide Church has recently repudiated some of these legalistic practices.[178]

---

[178]See Randy Frame, "Worldwide Church of God Edges Toward Orthodoxy," *Christianity Today* (9 November 1992): 58; Worldwide Church of God, *Summary of Doctrinal Statements*, 9-10, quoting *The Worldwide News* (letter from Personal Correspondence), 17 July 1989.

Part IV:
Sociological and Psychological Perspective on Cults and False Religions

I. The Place of Sociology in Cult Apologetics

A. *Cults must be defined theologically, not behaviorally; examining the group's doctrinal system is the only way to determine whether it is a cult.*

B. *Sociology is useful, but cannot be the basis on which cults are defined.*[179]

    1. Bad doctrine produces bad fruit behaviorally (e.g., Mark 7:7–13; Col. 2:20–23; 1 Tim. 4:1–5; 2 Peter 2:1–22; Rev. 2:14–5, 20, 24), which is as true for Christians as it is for cultists.

    2. As Van Baalen has well stated, "If practice follows from theory, if life is based upon teaching, it follows that the wrong doctrine will issue in the wrong attitude toward God and Christ, and consequently in warped and twisted Christian life."[180]

    3. Sociology and psychology—sciences that describe patterns of human behavior—may be able to provide information about behavioral characteristics that typify *some cults some of the time*.

    4. We first must determine if a group is cultic by examining its theology, and then we can examine its behavior to see how its beliefs "cash out" in practical life.

C. *Thus, this volume does not offer a sociological definition (since a meaningful one is impossible) but instead lists some of the behavioral characteristics that are sometimes found in cults (see section IV below).*

II. Limitations of the Social Science Perspective

A. *Sociology is descriptive, not prescriptive.*

    1. Sociology (and the social sciences generally) is designed to *describe* patterns of behavior and belief, not to say whether those behaviors and beliefs are good or bad, true or false.

---

[179]See the discussion on the problems with sociological definitions of cults in Part I, section III.A.3.
[180]Van Baalen, *Chaos of the Cults*, 352.

47

2. Sociology provides no basis for normative value judgments, or for evaluating the truth of religious claims.

   a. Value judgments and religious truth claims fall in the realm of theology, philosophy, and ethics—areas in which sociologists have no particular expertise.

   b. For example, sociologists may be able to describe patterns of authority found in certain religious groups but they cannot tell us (as sociologists) whether such practices are good, bad, or indifferent.

3. Naturally, individuals who are sociologists have the same right as any other individual to make value judgments about a group's religious beliefs and practices. The point is that sociological training does not give the judgment special weight and, therefore, such judgments should not be accorded expert status.

4. The problem is that sociologists frequently go beyond simple description and condemn groups without justifying a definite moral, ethical, and theological standard on which to base such judgment.

5. Unfortunately, the average reader of sociological literature may wrongly think that the sociologist's Ph.D. provides special qualifications to talk about the "evils" of cults.

B. *Because of their imprecision, sociological definitions may be falsely applied to legitimate Christian groups.*

1. For example, Conway and Siegelman point to the "ominous" similarities between the appeal of cult recruiters and the evangelistic techniques of Campus Crusade for Christ, Chuck Colson, and other evangelical Christians.[181]

2. "Indeed, [orthodox Christians] correctly perceived that . . . there was very little in the area of religious belief or practice that could not be classified as 'cultic' by some anti-cult spokesperson."[182]

3. Consider, for example, Enroth's "hallmarks of cultic conversion."[183] Note how virtually all of these apply or may apply to Christians.

   a. ". . . abandonment of a familiar lifestyle . . ."

      (1) Matthew 16:24—"If anyone would come after me, he must deny himself and take up his cross and follow me."

      (2) Ephesians 4:17—"You must no longer live as the Gentiles do."

   b. ". . . severing of ties with friends and families . . ."

      (1) Matthew 10:35–37—"For I have come to turn 'a man against his father, a daughter against her mother, a daughter-in-law against her mother-in-law—a man's enemies will be the members of his own household.' Anyone who loves his father or

---

[181]Conway and Siegelman, *Snapping*, 45.

[182]Shupe and Bromley, *The New Vigilantes,* 114.

[183]Enroth, *Youth, Brainwashing, and the Extremist Cults,* 12

mother more than me is not worthy of me; anyone who loves his son or daughter more than me is not worthy of me."

    (2) Mark 10:28–30—"Peter said to him, 'We have left everything to follow you!' 'I tell you the truth,' Jesus replied, 'no one who has left home or brothers or sisters or mother or father or children or fields for me and the gospel will fail to receive a hundred times as much in this present age (homes, brothers, sisters, mothers, children and fields—and with them, persecutions) and in the age to come, eternal life.'"

c. ". . . radical and sometimes sudden change in personality . . ."

Acts 9:20–21—"At once he [Paul] began to preach in the synagogues that Jesus is the Son of God. All those who heard him were astonished and asked, 'Isn't he the man who raised havoc in Jerusalem among those who call on this name? And hasn't he come here to take them as prisoners to the chief priests?'"

d. ". . . relinquishing of possessions . . ."

    (1) Matthew 5:42—"Give to the one who asks you, and do not turn away from the one who wants to borrow from you."

    (2) Acts 2:44—"All the believers were together and had everything in common. Selling their possessions and goods, they gave to anyone as he had need."

e. ". . . indoctrination with a new set of values, goals, and beliefs . . ."

    (1) Romans 12:2—"Do not conform any longer to the pattern of this world, but be transformed by the renewing of your mind."

    (2) Philippians 3:14—"I press on toward the goal to win the prize for which God has called me heavenward in Christ Jesus."

    (3) 2 Corinthians 10:5—"We demolish arguments and every pretension that sets itself up against the knowledge of God, and we take captive every thought to make it obedient to Christ."

f. ". . . assuming a totally new identity . . ."

    (1) Galatians 2:20—"I have been crucified with Christ and I no longer live, but Christ lives in me."

    (2) 2 Corinthians 5:17—"Therefore, if anyone is in Christ, he is a new creation; the old has gone, the new has come!"

g. ". . . including for some a new name . . ."

Acts 13:9 notes in passing, "Saul, who was also called Paul. . . ."[184]

h. ". . . isolation from the 'outside world with its attendant evil' . . ."

    (1) Romans 12:12—"Do not conform any longer to the pattern of this world, but be transformed by the renewing of your mind."

    (2) 1 John 2:15–16—"Do not love the world or anything in the world. If anyone loves the world, the love of the Father is not

---

[184]Many commentators note that "Saul" is called "Paul" after his conversion to Christ.

in him. For everything in the world—the cravings of sinful man, the lust of his eyes and the boasting of what he has and does—comes not from the Father but from the world."

4. From a survey of the above "hallmarks," it is clear that they apply to cults and Christians alike.

   a. The difference is that the cults base these practices on lies, whereas Christians ground them in the truth.

   b. The difference, then, is one of true vs. false religious claims—an issue which sociology cannot address.

C. *Sociological factors are subordinate to theological ones.*

   1. Sociologist Ronald Enroth has made the point cogently, even though he sometimes deviates from this principle in practice.

      a. Enroth says, "For the Christian the most significant component of a definition of a cult is theological in nature. This is so because basic issues of truth and error are involved. . . . The Christian must be able to distinguish truth from error."[185]

      b. Enroth also notes that "ultimately, any understanding of cultic systems necessarily requires examination of truth claims. Psychological and sociological explanations alone, as important and helpful as they may be, fail to fully explain the destructive elements in cultism. . . . The issue for the Christian, ultimately, is . . . whether what the converts are asked to believe and do is true."[186]

   2. Thus, even if it were possible to avoid the problems inherent in sociological analyses, the most important issues separating Christianity from the cults are theological and doctrinal.

III. Brainwashing, Mind Control, and Deprogramming

A. *Brief Statement of the Issue*

   1. A number of individuals and groups have claimed that some, most, or all cults practice "brainwashing" or "mind control."[187]

      a. Individuals

         Among the better-known individuals espousing the brainwashing/mind control model are Steven Hassan, a "highly regarded Jewish exit counselor from Boston";[188] Ted Patrick, author of *Let Our Children Go* and considered by many to be the "father" of

---

[185]Enroth, "What Is a Cult?" 15.

[186]Enroth, "Introduction," in *Evangelizing the Cults*, 12.

[187]Some make a distinction between mind control and brainwashing. The alleged distinction is discussed at point B.2 below.

[188]Alnor and Enroth, "Ethical Problems in Exit Counseling," 16. Hassan's *Combatting Cult Mind Control* is one of the most significant recent works written from the mind control perspective, and carries the

deprogramming, which began in the early 1970s;[189] Harvard psychologist John G. Clark; psychologist Margaret Singer; psychologist Michael Langone;[190] sociologist Ronald Enroth of Westmont College;[191] Flo Conway and Jim Siegelman, authors of *Snapping*; and apologist Jack Sparks, author of *The Mindbenders.*[192]

b. Organizations

Among the better-known organizations that have advocated the brainwashing/mind control model are: Citizens' Freedom Foundation—Cult Awareness Network; FREECOG (an anti-Children of God parents' group); Citizens Engaged in Reuniting Families; Citizens Engaged in Freeing Minds; Free Minds; and Individual Freedom Foundation.[193]

2. According to the mind control model, cults supposedly employ certain insidious techniques that enslave and control the minds of their followers. These are "extreme and unethical techniques of manipulation to recruit and assimilate members and to control members' thoughts, feelings, and behavior as a means of furthering the leader's goals."[194]

3. The alleged result of these mind control techniques is that the "victim's" free will is "subjugated." The alleged result of these mind control techniques is that the "victim's "free will" is subjugated." Indeed, "sharp, intelligent minds" are "turned to jelly."[195]

4. Supposedly, anyone is susceptible to these powerful mind control techniques.

B. Alleged Brainwashing/Mind Control Techniques

1. Brainwashing/mind control techniques are said to go beyond everyday persuasion, and may involve physical as well as psychological coercion to accomplish the desired goal.

2. Some distinguish between brainwashing and mind control.[196]

a. Brainwashing

---

endorsement of Margaret Singer, Ronald Enroth, and other important researchers who affirm the mind control position.

[189]Ibid.

[190]E.g., Michael Langone, of the American Family Foundation, *Destructive Cultism: Questions and Answers* (1982); *Cults: What Every Parent Should Know* (1988).

[191]E.g., *Youth, Brainwashing, and the Extremist Cults*, 131. Enroth's advocacy of the mind control model is discussed in Robert Passantino and Gretchen Passantino, "Overcoming the Bondage of Victimization: A Critical Evaluation of Cult Mind Control and Exit Counseling," *Cornerstone* vol. 22, issue 102-103 (Spring 1994), 34.

[192]Sparks, *The Mindbenders*, 16.

[193]Enroth lists some of these groups in *Youth, Brainwashing, and the Extremist Cults*, 190.

[194]Joan Carol Ross and Michael Langone, *Cults: What Parents Should Know* (Weston, Mass.: American Family Foundation, 1988), 20.

[195]Enroth, *Youth, Brainwashing, and the Extremist Cults*, 156; Ross and Langone, *Cults: What Parents Should Know*, 19.

[196]See, for example, Steven Hassan, *Combatting Cult Mind Control* (Rochester, Ver.: Park Street Press, 1990), 55-56.

      (1) Brainwashing is said to be more overtly coercive, often involving physical torture, starvation, and abuse (e.g., POWs).

      (2) In CIA experiments it involved hallucinogenic drugs and electroshock therapy.[197]

      (3) In cults it allegedly takes the form of inadequate diet and minimal sleep.

      (4) The idea behind such sensory deprivation is that it supposedly makes people manipulable and unable to think for themselves.[198]

    b. Mind control

      (1) Mind control is "more subtle and sophisticated" and "involves little or no overt physical abuse. Instead, *hypnotic processes* are combined with *group dynamics* to create a potent indoctrination effect."[199]

      (2) It is claimed that irresistible social pressures are brought to bear on the individual, which force conformity to the cult.

      (3) Hypnotism is a popular technique purportedly used in cultic mind control.[200]

      The cults use hypnosis to increase the effectiveness of their mind control techniques.[201] For example, ex-Unification Church member Richard Greenwald stated, "I learned to hypnotize people and went out to witness, bringing in new people. In Berkeley we were bringing thirty new people every day. And they were hooked by that first supper and lecture."[202] Similarly, "Ted Patrick claims that the Unification church leaders use 'spot hypnosis' to snare recruits and pass the secrets of the technique down through their lieutenants to street witnessing teams."[203]

    c. In either case, the techniques are regarded as subversive and accomplish the same effect. The mind control method is simply the more subtle and typically less physical of the two.

  3. These techniques are supposedly so powerful that no one is safe from them.

---

[197]Ibid., 189. See also Stephen Budansky, Erica Goode, and Ted Gest, "The Cold War Experiments," *U. S. New and World Report* 116, no. 3 (24 January 1994).

[198]Anthony and Robbins, "Law, Social Science and the 'Brainwashing' Exception to the First Amendment," *Behavioral Sciences and the Law* 10, no. 1, "Cults and the Law" (Winter 1992): 13; Enroth, *Youth, Brainwashing, and the Extremist Cults,* 160-61.

[199]Hassan, *Combatting Cult Mind Control,* 56 (emphasis in the original).

[200]Ibid., 69.

[201]Ibid., 67.

[202]Shupe and Bromley, *The New Vigilantes,* 158.

[203]David Bromley and Anson Shupe, *Strange Gods: The Great American Cult Scare* (Boston: Beacon, 1981), 93. Note, however, that Ted Patrick also claimed under oath that the Unificationists emanate invisible energy rays through their fingertips.

a. Even young people with "relatively normal, healthy personalities upon entering cultic groups" can be victimized by mind control.[204]

b. According to Ted Patrick, *everybody* is vulnerable to mind control techniques.[205]

c. Hassan states, "Anyone . . . can be recruited to a cult. The major variable is . . . the cult recruiter's level of skill."[206]

d. Proponents of the mind control model say that the victim is not responsible for what has happened; because mind control is such a "subtle but powerful force over which [the victim] had little or no control," victims "need not feel either guilt or shame because of their experience."[207]

C. Alleged Results of Brainwashing

1. The mind control victim is said to be unable to exercise free choice.[208] The free will has been put into "cold storage,"[209] and "the will to be self-determining is absent."[210]

   a. Mind control theorists say that "the aftermath of brainwashing is a severe impairment of autonomy and [of] ability to think independently which induces a subject's unyielding compliance and the rupture of past connections, affiliations and associations."[211]

   b. Some have compared this to a robot or zombie-like state.[212] Mind controlled cultists are "puppets on strings"[213] who render blind and slavish obedience to the dictates of the cult.

2. Because mind control victims are said to be unable to leave the cult on their own volition, intervention is deemed necessary.

   They must be "deprogrammed" or undergo "exit counseling," during which the grip of so-called cultic mind control is broken through a variety of confrontational methods.[214]

---

[204]Enroth, *Youth, Brainwashing, and the Extremist Cults*, 156.

[205]Shupe and Bromley, *The New Vigilantes*, 72.

[206]Hassan, *Combatting Cult Mind Control*, 77.

[207]Paul Martin, "Wellspring's Approach to Cult Rehab," cited in Passantino and Passantino, "Overcoming the Bondage of Victimization," 32.

[208]John L. Young and Ezra E. H. Griffith, "A Critical Evaluation of Coercive Persuasion as Used in the Assessment of Cults," *Behavioral Sciences and the Law* 10, no. 1 (Winter 1992): 89.

[209]Ted Patrick, cited in Bromley and Shupe, *Strange Gods*, 180-81.

[210]Enroth, *Youth, Brainwashing, and the Extremist Cults*, 193.

[211]Anthony and Robbins, "Law, Social Science and the 'Brainwashing' Exception," 13; citing the court case Peterson v. Sorlien, 1980.

[212]John Dart, "Deprogrammers' 'Rescuer' Status, Ideology Increasingly Rebuffed," *Los Angeles Times* (23 January 1982), part IA, p. 2, quoting deprogrammer Cliff Daniels.

[213]Sparks, *The Mindbenders*, 18.

[214]Enroth, *Youth, Brainwashing, and the Extremist Cults*, 195, citing Kevin Gilmartin. Exit counseling and deprogramming are discussed at point F below. The distinction between deprogramming and exit counseling is discussed at point G below.

D. Proof Given for the Brainwashing Theory

(Note: As will become clear, I totally reject the brainwashing/mind control model. The arguments below are those commonly given by advocates of the mind control theory.)

1. Studies of brainwashing performed by Chinese Communists and the CIA are used to argue that brainwashing is real and powerful.

   a. Robert Lifton did pioneering research on brainwashing practiced by the Chinese Communists on American POWs in Korea (see his *Thought Reform and the Psychology of Totalism*).

   b. Lifton stated, "It is probably fair to say that the Chinese Communist prison and revolutionary university produce about as thoroughly controlled a group environment as has ever existed."[215]

   c. The cults are said to use the same well-established techniques of thought reform.[216]

      (1) Ex-Unificationist Steven Hassan claims that the techniques and processes cited in Lifton's book "were almost identical" to the ones used in the Unification Church.[217]

      (2) Indeed, Hassan says that the cults today have perfected the older techniques: "Destructive cults today have the added advantage of the thirty years of psychological research and techniques since Mao, making their mind control programs much more effective and dangerous. Hypnotic processes, for example, are much more significant in modern mind control."[218]

   d. Hassan says that CIA research involving "experimentation with LSD, hypnosis, and electroshock therapy," also demonstrates the reality of thought control.[219]

2. Testimonies of ex-cult members are also offered as evidence of brainwashing.

   a. Consider, for example, the testimony of ex-Unificationist Christopher Edwards.

      (1) Edwards says he was brainwashed by the Unification Church.

      (2) In his book *Crazy for God*, Edwards describes "the sinister indoctrination process" by which he was "transformed from an intelligent, independent human being into a completely subservient disciple" of Rev. Moon.[220]

---

[215]Robert J. Lifton, *Thought Reform and the Psychology of Totalism: A Study of "Brainwashing" in China* (New York: Norton, 1961), 420.

[216]Sparks, *The Mindbenders*, 17.

[217]Hassan, *Combatting Cult Mind Control*, 28.

[218]Ibid., 67.

[219]See, for example, Hassan, *Combatting Cult Mind Control*, 189. The Passantinos discuss the CIA experiments in "Overcoming the Bondage of Victimization," 33, 37

[220]Christopher Edwards, *Crazy for God* (Englewood Cliffs, N.J.: Prentice-Hall, 1979), foreword, ix-x.

(3) Edwards describes the details of his deprogramming, performed by Ted Patrick.[221]

(4) Edwards compares the mind control techniques used on him to the techniques used by the Chinese in the 1950s.[222]

b. Proponents of the mind control model say that researchers have found brainwashing to be a recurring theme among cult members.

(1) Some professional psychologists, psychiatrists, and sociologists argue that testimonies like Edwards's (2.a above) are not isolated.

(2) Sociologist Ronald Enroth recounts the case histories of many "victims" of cultic thought control in his *Youth, Brainwashing, and the Extremist Cults.*

(3) Enroth speaks of "thousands of parents and ex-cult members" who provide consistent and truthful testimony to the fact of brainwashing. To deny the truth of brainwashing is to accuse these sincere parents and ex-cultists of being "deluded" and of "misrepresenting the facts."[223]

(4) Enroth believes that when the same stories come up over and over, they have a "ring of truth" to them.[224]

E. The Case Against the Mind Control Theory

Among academic sociologists, "the brainwashing/thought reform explanation is not even discussed anymore at sociology meetings, it's so discredited."[225] Below are some of the main reasons why the mind control paradigm is no longer entertained by serious social scientists.

1. Classic brainwashing performed under ideal conditions simply did not work.

a. Modern advocates of the brainwashing and mind control position invariably cite the brainwashing experiments of the Communist Chinese and the CIA,[226] but they fail to discuss one rather important fact: the Chinese and CIA experiments were dismal failures![227]

"For example, Alan Scheflin and Edward Opton, in their book *The Mind Manipulators,* point out that of over 3,500 American POWs captured during the Korean War only about 50 ever made pro-Communist statements and only about 25 refused to be repatriated

---

[221]Ibid., 209-27.

[222]Ibid., 231.

[223]Enroth, *Youth, Brainwashing, and the Extremist Cults,* 193.

[224]Ronald Enroth, *Churches That Abuse* (Grand Rapids: Zondervan, 1992), 32.

[225]Sociologist Anson Shupe of Indiana/Purdue University, quoted in John Trott, "The Pain of Leaving, the Pain of Being Left: An Interview with Sociologist Anson Shupe," *Cornerstone* vol. 22, issue 102-103 (Spring 1994), 44.

[226]Hassan, *Combatting Cult Mind Control,* 38, 189.

[227]Anthony and Robbins, "Law, Social Science and the 'Brainwashing' Exception," 16.

when the war ended. The authors compare those figures (50 out of 3,500, or about 1%) with the enlistment in the Confederate Army of Union Soldiers captured during the Civil War: 2%, or roughly a 2 to 1 ratio."[228]

b. At most the Chinese were able to effect "trivial acts of collaboration," but were unable to cause any substantive shift in a person's thinking.[229]

c. Likewise, the CIA abandoned its experiments on brainwashing because they were so ineffective.[230]

2. If the Communist Chinese and the CIA could not make brainwashing work, it is difficult to believe that a cultist could.

a. Remember Lifton's observation: "It is probably fair to say that the Chinese Communist prison and revolutionary university produce about as thoroughly controlled a group environment as has ever existed."[231] Yet, as noted above, the program did not work even in this highly controlled environment.

b. If the Communists and CIA could not make it work, how can the cults?

"It stretches one's credulity to believe that what highly trained and technologically supported CIA, Russian, Korean, and Chinese experts could not accomplish under extremes of mental, emotional, and physical abuse, self-styled modern messiahs like David Koresh (high school dropout), Charles Manson (grade school dropout), and Hare Krishna founder Prabhupada (self-educated) accomplished on a daily basis and on a massive scale with control methods measurably inferior to those of POW camp torturers. Do we really believe that what the Soviets couldn't do to Aleksandr Solzhenitsyn during years of forced labor and torture in the Gulag, Sun Myung Moon could have done by 'love bombing' for one week at an idyllic wilderness retreat?"[232]

3. The claim that cults use hypnotism to augment the efficacy of classic brainwashing techniques is absurd.

a. As noted above, classic brainwashing is ineffective. Therefore, there is nothing for the supposed hypnotic techniques to "augment."

b. Hypnotism is far less effective than commonly thought.

The *Encyclopedia Britannica* notes, "It now seems quite unlikely that the hypnotized person can transcend his waking potential in physical strength, perceptiveness, learning ability, and productiv-

---

[228]Bromley and Shupe, *Strange Gods*, 99.

[229]Anthony and Robbins, "Law, Social Science and the 'Brainwashing' Exception," 16.

[230]Passantino and Passantino, "Overcoming the Bondage of Victimization," 37.

[231]Lifton, *Thought Reform*, 420.

[232]Passantino and Passantino, "Overcoming the Bondage of Victimization," 33. Richardson makes the same point (45-46).

ity. Similarly, it seems most improbable that hypnotized people can be compelled to do what they would be most unwilling to do in the waking state."[233]

c. The description of hypnotism allegedly practiced by cults sometimes reads more like science fiction than science. For example, famed deprogrammer Ted Patrick claimed under oath that the Moonies emanate invisible energy rays through their fingertips.[234]

4. Even if classic brainwashing were effective it would not prove the mind control model.

a. On the one hand, mind control advocates distinguish between brainwashing and mind control.

(1) The brainwashing practiced by the Chinese Communists regularly involved torture and severe physical depletion, but few would seriously compare, for example, the Krishna devotee's Hindu vegetarian diet with starvation in a POW camp.[235]

(2) Because of this obvious difference, Hassan states that "the two processes [i.e., brainwashing and mind control] are quite different and should not be confused."[236]

b. On the other hand, mind control advocates contradict themselves by citing studies of classic brainwashing as proof of their mind control model.

Hassan states that "the techniques and processes used by the Communist Chinese . . . to brainwash prisoners during the 1950s" were "almost identical" to "the processes we used in the Moonies."[237]

c. Since mind control techniques do not rely on physical coercion while brainwashing techniques do, it is difficult to see how brainwashing experiments could provide the theoretical underpinnings for the mind control model.

5. The high attrition/defection rate in cults argues against the brainwashing model.

a. "Leaving religious groups and movements is as important as joining and about as frequent."[238]

---

233 *Macropaedia*, 9:138.

234 Bromley and Shupe, *Strange Gods*, 93.

235 Oddly, Singer is one who does try to argue for just such a similarity. Anthony and Robbins state, "In the communist POW context, physical debilitation was so severe that one-third of the POWs died, yet Schein found that among the survivors, the clarity of their thought processes had not been diminished. Singer (1983) testified that serious debilitation and resulting impairment can be produced by a Hindu vegetarian diet and related physical practices" (Anthony and Robbins, "Law, Social Science and the 'Brainwashing' Exception," 17).

236 Hassan, *Combatting Cult Mind Control*, 55. See the discussion of mind control vs. brainwashing at point B.2 above.

237 Ibid., 28.

238 James R. Richardson, "Conversion, Brainwashing, and Deprogramming in New Religions," *Update: A Quarterly Journal on New Religious Movements* 6, no. 1 (March 1982): 37.

b. Numerous studies have shown that cults—*especially the ones most often accused of mind control*—experience high turnover rates.[239]

Most of the defections come from natural attrition; that is, people who simply leave on their own, without any outside intervention.

c. It is impossible to reconcile the notion of omnipotent, mind enslaving techniques with the fact that people frequently leave these groups without kidnapping, deprogramming, or any outside intervention whatever.

   (1) For example, according to one study, "the first graduating class from Moon's Unification Theological Seminary in Barrytown, New York, whose students represent the elite of Unification Church members, witnessed a seventeen percent defection rate soon after graduation."[240]

   (2) Among rank and file cult members the drop out rate is higher still.

   Citing Eileen Barker's work the Passantinos observe: "Natural attrition (people leaving the group without specific intervention) was much higher than the self-claimed 65 percent deprogramming success figure! It is far more likely a new convert would leave the cult within the first year of his membership than it is that he would become a long-term member."[241]

6. The testimonies of ex-members who claim to have been brainwashed are usually tainted by their deprogramming experience or by exposure to anticult brainwashing literature.

   a. Trudy Solomon demonstrated in a well-designed study that those who left the Unification Church without the intervention of deprogrammers were much more likely to admit that they joined and remained in the group voluntarily. Conversely, deprogrammees were much more likely to attribute their involvement in the cult to brainwashing.[242]

   b. Solomon states, "Contact with the anticult movement influences the degree to which one relies on explanations of brainwashing and mind control to account for attraction to and membership in the church. Thus, belief in such explanations increased if an ex-mem-

---

[239]Richardson, "Conversion, Brainwashing, and Deprogramming," 45; Bromley and Shupe, *Strange Gods*, 125; Anthony and Robbins, "New Religions, Families, and 'Brainwashing,'" 271; Melton, *Encyclopedic Handbook of Cults in America*, 13, 18; Eileen Barker, "From Sects to Society: A Methodological Programme," in *New Religious Movements: A Perspective for Understanding Society*, Studies in Religion and Society, vol. 3 (New York: Edwin Mellen, 1982), 13.

[240]Bromley and Shupe, *Strange Gods*, 109-10.

[241]Passantino and Passantino, "Overcoming the Bondage of Victimization," 37.

[242]E.g., Trudy Solomon, "Integrating the 'Moonie' Experience: A Survey of Ex-Members of the Unification Church," in *In Gods We Trust*, 279, 288, 292. Richardson discusses this study on p. 47.

ber was involved in anti-Unification-church groups and getting others out, or if his or her parents were so involved."[243]

c. In contrast to Solomon's study, consider the "case histories" given in Enroth's *Youth, Brainwashing, and the Extremist Cults.*

    (1) Note that all of his interviewees had been deprogrammed, many by Ted Patrick.

    (2) It is hardly surprising that these deprogrammed individuals would trust the "expert" opinions of Patrick and Enroth, and read brainwashing back into their earlier involvement in the cult.

7. The brainwashing/mind control theory is a convenient way of absolving parents and children of responsibility for actions freely chosen.[244]

a. Parents usually have certain expectations for their child's future; if a child deviates significantly from parental goals (e.g., becoming a flower-selling Moonie instead of an upscale lawyer), the parents might have to face the fact that the child has repudiated the parents' value system.

b. Mind control provides an easy way for parents to absolve themselves of failure. After all, since cultic mind control techniques are overwhelmingly powerful, and since anyone is vulnerable, it is the cult's fault and not the parents' that their child was psychologically kidnapped by the cult.

c. As Anthony and Robbins observe, "Our children only *appear* to be repudiating our values because they have been driven crazy by evil men. In this way parents are able to absolve themselves of responsibility for their children's defection."[245]

d. As in the case of parents, the ex-cultist may use the mind control explanation to rationalize away responsibility for having been "duped" by the cult: the ex-cultist was a victim of powers quite beyond his or her own control.

F. *"Deprogramming" and "Exit Counseling" Defined*

1. The term *deprogramming* was first coined by Ted Patrick in the early 1970s.[246]

2. "Deprogramming is a process in which allegedly mind controlled or 'programmed' converts to cults are dramatically 'rescued' (often abducted) and presented with arguments against their continued participation. Such arguments usually involve allegations that converts

---

[243]Solomon, "Integrating the 'Moonie' Experience," 288. Melton also makes this point well in *Encyclopedic Handbook of Cults in America*, 354–55.

[244]Eileen Barker, *New Religious Movements: A Practical Introduction* (London: Her Majesty's Stationery Office, 1989), 17.

[245]Anthony and Robbins, "New Religions, Families, and 'Brainwashing,'" 270.

[246]Alnor and Enroth, "Ethical Problems in Exit Counseling," 17.

have been brainwashed and thus that they are being held in cults against their will."[247]

3. The word *deprogramming* has been applied loosely by some, both to coercive, forcible abductions of cultists and to attempts at persuasion in which the cultist voluntarily participates.[248]

4. Today it is fashionable to distinguish between "deprogramming" and "exit counseling."

   a. Those making the distinction reserve the word *deprogramming* for situations involving abductions, in which the cultist is held against his will.

   b. *Exit counseling* is the expression used to describe the non-coercive variety of persuading cultists to leave their groups.[249]

G. Comparison Between Deprogramming and Exit Counseling

1. The most obvious difference between deprogramming and exit counseling is that deprogramming—by definition—is performed against the cultist's will.

2. Both models assume the truth of the brainwashing/mind control explanation of cultic involvement.

   a. They both assume that cultists have no free will to leave the cult until they have "snapped out of" their mind-controlled state through the deprogramming/exit counseling techniques.

   b. As noted above, the brainwashing/mind control model is hopelessly flawed. Therefore, both exit counseling and deprogramming are built on the same untenable foundation.

3. Both in deprogramming and in exit counseling, the goal is to bring the person back to a religiously "neutral" position.[250]

H. Arguments Against the Deprogramming/Exit Counseling Theory

1. Forced deprogramming is unethical.

   a. Abducting people because of their religious beliefs is a violation of the First Amendment, which guarantees freedom of religion.

      (1) Deprogrammers seek a loophole in the First Amendment guarantee of religious freedom, arguing that the Constitutional protections assume *voluntary* participation in a religious group.[251]

      (2) However, courts have almost always ruled against the deprogrammers in such cases, in part because the mind control theory does not have sufficient scientific warrant.[252]

---

[247]Anthony and Robbins, "Law, Social Science and the 'Brainwashing' Exception," 6-7.

[248]Bromley and Shupe, *Strange Gods*, 182-83.

[249]Alnor and Enroth, "Ethical Problems in Exit Counseling," 17.

[250]Passantino and Passantino, "Overcoming the Bondage of Victimization," 32, 38.

[251]Anthony and Robbins, "New Religions, Families, and 'Brainwashing,'" 264.

[252]Space does not permit analysis of the many court cases on this subject. Of the large body of literature on this subject, the interested reader may wish to consult the following as a quick sampling: Anthony

b. Abducting people even for non-religious reasons is kidnapping, which is immoral and illegal.

Note that the individuals who are abducted are often responsible adults. Thus, from a legal perspective their parents or relatives—who typically arrange for the abduction—have no legal jurisdiction over their activities.

c. Deprogramming perpetrates violence often as bad and sometimes worse than any cult.

    (1) "Ironically, in view of the allegations of coercion in cults, such rescued converts are frequently physically confined during the deprogramming process, and the methods of persuasion are sometimes harsh and confrontational."[253]

    (2) "A good case can be made that the trauma and psychic conflict it induces can conceivably *cause* mental illness if not exacerbate such problems."[254]

    (3) Though deprogrammers rationalize such inhuman treatment by declaring that it is "for the cultist's own good," such abusive treatment is inherently reprehensible.

    (4) Even in cases of allegedly "successful" deprogrammings, the deprogrammers should remember that Paul condemned those who "do evil that good may result" (Rom. 3:8).

2. Deprogramming is ineffective.

  a. While advocates of the deprogramming position have claimed high rates of success, studies show that *natural attrition rates* actually are higher than the success rate achieved through deprogramming.

  b. It is tragic that fees of $20,000 per case are not uncommon,[255] particularly when there is a greater chance of the loved one leaving with no intervention than through deprogramming.

3. Salvation, not religious neutrality, is the proper goal.

  a. Both in deprogramming and in exit counseling, the goal is simply to get the cultist to renounce his or her involvement in the cult.

  b. Exit counselors seek to bring the person to a place of "religious neutrality."

---

and Robbins, "Law, Social Science and the 'Brainwashing' Exception"; Young and Griffith, "Evaluation of Coercive Persuasion," 95-96; Richardson, "Conversion, Brainwashing, and Deprogramming," 44-47; Bromley and Shupe, *Strange Gods*, 177-81; Shupe and Bromley, *The New Vigilantes*, 185; Tucker, *Another Gospel*, 28.

  [253]Anthony and Robbins, "Law, Social Science and the 'Brainwashing' Exception," 6-7.

  [254]Bromley and Shupe, *Strange Gods*, 202. See also Anthony and Robbins, "New Religions, Families, and 'Brainwashing,'" 272-73; Melton, *Encyclopedic Handbook of Cults* in America, 354.

  [255]Alnor and Enroth, "Ethical Problems in Exit Counseling," 15. The Cult Awareness Network has informally set guidelines for exit counselors, including fee schedules. "Reasonable" fees for cases range from $400 to $1000 per day, depending on the "experience" of the deprogrammer (16).

      c. Religious neutrality, however, is a myth.

         Jesus stated, "He who is not with me is against me" (Matt. 12:30).

      d. The Christian must seek to win the lost for Christ—be they cultist or not.

         A person who fancies himself or herself "religiously neutral" is just as lost as anyone in a cult.

  4. The methods of deprogramming and exit counseling contradict the mind control theory on which they are based.

      a. Deprogrammers and exit counselors assume that the cultist is brainwashed and consequently unable to freely choose to leave the cult. Yet, they seek to change the "brainwashed" mind of the cultist by presenting rational arguments against the cult!

      b. If the cultist has been turned into a zombie by the cult, it is hard to understand how he or she could respond to the reasoned appeals of the deprogrammer.

  5. Cultists are spiritually blinded but not mind controlled.

      a. Cultists are not coerced through mind control to reject the gospel. They have willingly rejected the truth and are responsible for their choice (2 Thess. 2:10).

      b. Spiritual blindness is true of all unbelievers (2 Cor. 4:4), and is not the result of mind control technology. This blindness is as true for the unsaved sociologist and deprogrammer as it is for the Moonie.

      c. God has provided a cure for this blindness: the gospel.

         Cultists are capable of understanding and processing the implications of the gospel. They will be cured of their blindness only if they believe this gospel.

IV. Sociological Characteristics/Practices of Cults—Real and Imagined

A. *Authoritarianism*[256]

  1. Description

      a. Jack Sparks, author of *The Mindbenders*, lists as characteristic of cults "a dominant leader who is considered the sole interpreter of God's truth."[257]

      b. Such leaders are sometimes described by their followers as "new prophets, apostles, or messiahs."[258]

---

[256]Martin, *Kingdom of the Cults*, 28; McDowell and Stewart, *The Deceivers*, 21.

[257]Sparks, *The Mindbenders*, 24.

[258]McDowell and Stewart, *The Deceivers*, 21.

    c. The leaders tend to be isolated, both from other religious groups and from the society at large.[259]

2. Examples

    a. Unification Church

       (1) Moon describes himself as the "True Parent," to whom obedience must be given.[260]

       (2) Moon stated, "This master of yours has disciples who are ready to sacrifice their lives for this great cause. . . . Out of all the saints sent by God, I think I am the most successful one . . . as it now stands. . . . You can trust me as your leader. . . . I am a thinker, I am your brain."[261]

    b. Boston Church of Christ

       (1) Ronald Enroth mentions the Boston Church of Christ movement under the leadership of Kip McKean as an example of authoritarianism.[262]

       (2) The Boston Church practices a kind of discipleship "in which the personal life of every believer is controlled by a discipler who is over that person. There is a discipler over every discipler, a hierarchy of disciplers working its way up to the top. Through this the church maintains control of each person."[263]

3. Qualifications to the Above Description

    a. Sometimes cultural factors should be taken into account.

       (1) The Unification Church in particular has been highly criticized for being authoritarian and controlling, which indeed it is.

       (2) However, sometimes cultural factors need to be taken into account.

       For example, the arranged marriage ceremonies performed by Moon might be quite acceptable in Korean and other eastern cultures.[264]

    b. Some would regard the Christian church as "authoritarian" and "totalistic."

       (1) Anthony and Robbins claim that Christians in the first century could be seen in this way.[265]

---

[259]Ibid., 21-22.

[260]Enroth, "What Is a Cult?" 17-18.

[261]Moon, quoted in Enroth, *Youth, Brainwashing, and the Extremist Cults*, 182.

[262]Enroth, *Churches That Abuse*, 116.

[263]Jim Bjornstad, "Success at What Price? The Boston (Church of Christ) Movement," *Christian Research Journal* (Winter 1993): 27.

[264]Tucker, *Another Gospel*, 256.

[265]Anthony and Robbins, "New Religions, Families, and 'Brainwashing,'" 267.

(2) Indeed, Paul was totalistic when he said that we should "take captive every thought to make it obedient to Christ" (2 Cor. 10:5).

(3) Jesus Christ himself was totalistic when he said, "If anyone would come after me, he must deny himself and take up his cross and follow me" (Matt. 16:24; Mark 8:34; Luke 9:23).

(4) In a society that has become increasingly relativistic, a Christian church that would dare to excommunicate someone based on an absolute standard of right and wrong could be perceived as authoritarian.

(5) The problem with cultic authoritarianism is that fallible, sinful cult leaders demand absolute allegiance to themselves and to their unbiblical standards rather than to Jesus Christ and his standards.

B. Psychological Manipulation

1. Description

   a. Cults and cult leaders apply social pressure to ensure conformity to the standards of the group.

   b. Sometimes guilt is used as an effective weapon of manipulation.

   c. Enroth points out that a guilty person is more manipulable. He states, "The rigorous standards [of the cult] can seldom be met; the individual nearly always falls short and is left remorseful and repentant (and thus more easily manipulable)."[266]

   d. Fear of divine retribution for failure to submit to the cult is also a powerful inducement to obedience.

2. Examples

   a. Alamo Christian Foundation

      Enroth says that the Alamo group effects mind control through fear by preaching a wrathful god.[267]

   b. Jehovah's Witnesses

      (1) Fear of disfellowshipping is a painful inducement to remain in the Watchtower movement.

      (2) Jehovah's Witnesses are taught that in order to avoid destruction at Armageddon they must remain within Jehovah's chosen organization.

3. Qualifications to the Above Description

   a. *All* groups apply various social pressures to conform. This is true of mainline churches as well as of non-religious institutions such as the military.

---

[266]Enroth, *Youth, Brainwashing, and the Extremist Cults*, 160.

[267]Enroth, *Youth, Brainwashing, and the Extremist Cults*, 161. The notion of "mind control" is refuted in Part IV, section III.E. Nonetheless, Enroth is correct when he says that the cults use fear to persuade people to remain in the group.

b. One might counter that cults apply excessive pressure. However, it may be a subjective judgment as to when the line between acceptable and excessive pressure is crossed.

c. There is a legitimate sense in which people ought to fear God's judgment.

    (1) Scripture does speak of God's wrath against sin,[268] and Jesus spoke a great deal about hell (e.g., Matt. 25:41, 46).

    (2) The problem with cultic fear is that it is not based on the truth. People held in bondage to cultic fear believe God's judgment will fall if they are unfaithful to the (unbiblical) expectations of the cult.

    (3) The solution to cultic fear is the *truth*, which Jesus said will set people free (John 8:32).

C. Stripping of Past Associations, Particularly with Family

1. Description

a. Some cults demand that the person renounce past associations, particularly parents and other family members.[269]

b. This may be done to ensure total allegiance to the cult, which is portrayed as the person's "new family."

    (1) Parents and other family members are often the ones who most oppose involvement in a cult, so it is not surprising that cults would urge their members to avoid contact with family.

    (2) "Parents are referred to as 'the devil in disguise' and relatives are considered to be 'just flesh relationships.'"[270]

    (3) Sometimes cultists are given a new name to reinforce the act of severing ties.[271]

    (4) Parents have formed anticult groups to "rescue" their children from "mind controlling" cults, which have snatched their children from them.

    Much of the deprogramming activity has taken place at the urging of concerned parents.

2. Examples

a. Children of God

Children of God leaders were known to discourage a member's contact with parents. Sometimes they would allow contact with parents only as long as the parents were a source of money or

---

[268]For example, Rom. 1:18; 2:5, 8; 5:9; Eph. 5:6; Col. 3:6; 1 Thess. 1:10; 2:16; 5:9; Rev. 6:16-17; 11:18; 14:10, 19; 15:1, 7; 16:1, 19; 19:15.

[269]Enroth, *Youth, Brainwashing, and the Extremist Cults*, 12

[270]Ibid., 174.

[271]Ibid., 163. See also point J below on the use of familial imagery.

material goods. When it became apparent that family members were not winnable to the cult, it would cut off all contact.

b. The Hare Krishnas, Unification Church, the Way International, and Branch Davidians have all encouraged breaking ties with past family and friends in many instances.

3. Qualifications to the Above Description

a. In some circumstances, renouncing past associations is biblical.

(1) Many Christians have experienced opposition from parents and other family members upon accepting Christ as Lord.

(2) Christians should try lovingly to evangelize their unsaved family members. In some circumstances, however, the hostility may be so great that the only practical alternative is to sever contact until (hopefully) a more opportune time.

b. Jesus expected his followers to be more devoted to him than to their own families (Matt. 10:35–37).

c. Children join cults often to escape a family that is *already* dysfunctional. Their membership in the cult is the result, not the cause, of family dysfunction.

Anthony and Robbins state: "In our view, the upsurge of cults is indeed associated with trends undermining familial solidarity in America, but cultism is more a consequence than a cause of such trends. . . . Available research is [thus] not consistent with a model of psychological kidnapping in which an otherwise dutiful and conformist young citizen is hypnotically overwhelmed and imprisoned in a deviant lifestyle which would otherwise be anathema."[272]

D. Sensory Deprivation

1. Description

a. Enroth states, "All ex-members of extremist cults report having experienced some kind of sensory deprivation—usually food or sleep. [This makes] a person even more vulnerable to indoctrination."[273]

b. People in cults are said to be often so incapacitated and disoriented by "sleep deprivation, bad nutrition, exhausting labor, emotional manipulation and seductive pseudosolidarity"[274] that they no longer have the mental ability to objectively evaluate their participation in the group.

c. Enroth talks about the starchy, low protein diet and four to five hours of sleep a night, which is said to wear down psychological defenses and make people more vulnerable to indoctrination.

---

[272]Anthony and Robbins, "New Religions, Families, and 'Brainwashing,'" 271.

[273]Enroth, *Youth, Brainwashing, and the Extremist Cults*, 160-61.

[274]Anthony and Robbins, "Law, Social Science and the 'Brainwashing' Exception," 8. This is not the view of Anthony and Robbins, but it is one commonly advanced to justify activities such as deprogramming.

    d. Conway and Siegelman contend that after consistent indoctrination, lack of food and sleep, minimal protein in the diet, etc., an "explosive overstimulation or emotional collapse" takes place.

      (1) "An individual's personality may come apart," which Conway and Siegelman call "snapping."

      (2) The sensory deprivation that cultists experienced before this time contributes to this snapping event.[275]

2. Alleged Examples

    a. People's Temple

    Living conditions in Jim Jones's Jonestown colony were terrible: many basic necessities of food and hygiene were missing or sorely lacking.[276]

    b. Unification Church

    "Individual resistance was critically lowered by a lack of even minimally adequate nutrition. For example: 'There was very little protein in the diet. The food was almost totally carbohydrates (cookies, ice cream, coke, peanut butter and jelly sandwiches). On Sunday you might get a drumstick.'"[277]

3. Qualifications to the Above Description

    a. Enroth says that sensory deprivation characterizes so-called "extremist" cults. Whether or not it is truly characteristic of "extremist" groups, it certainly does not characterize the mainline cults, such as Mormons and Jehovah's Witnesses. If sensory deprivation is practiced at all it is the exception and not the rule.

    b. Claims of sensory deprivation may be exaggerated.

    Bromley and Shupe refute the notion that Unification Church members were controlled by diet and lack of sleep:

    "New members were supposed to be kept lethargic and subservient because of inadequate protein-poor diets, but we ate their food, often dropping in unannounced in cities such as Arlington, Houston, New York, and San Francisco, and found it nutritious. Instead of minimal sleep designed to dull members into suggestibility, we found the same five- or six-hours-a-night regimen familiar to millions of college students, interspersed with occasional naps. Moonies were supposed to be kept in states of mental confusion by continually poring over Moon's scripture *Divine Principle*, but in moments of relaxation we found them reading Tolkien's *The Lord of the Rings* and the potboiler biography *Jackie O!* Every working moment was supposed to be consecrated and devoted to the sole

---

[275]Conway and Siegelman, *Snapping,* 57, 135.

[276]Sparks, *The Mindbenders,* 266.

[277]Shupe and Bromley, *The New Vigilantes,* 157.

purpose of ushering in the kingdom of God on earth, but they spent Sunday afternoons at the movies seeing *Star Wars* and *O, God!*"[278]

c. There is a sense in which certain perfectly orthodox groups practice "sensory deprivation."

  (1) Christian monastic communities historically have practiced varying degrees of asceticism. This has included a very modest diet and limited sleep (e.g., for observing the "canonical hours" of prayer).

  (2) Jesus himself fasted for a full forty days (Luke 4:2).

  (3) Of course, there is no spiritual virtue in the voluntary self-deprivation practiced by cults because it is not based on true godliness (1 Tim. 4:1–8).

d. Without proof it cannot be assumed that lack of sleep and poor diet make a person more vulnerable to indoctrination.[279] Is it not equally reasonable to assume that poor diet and lack of sleep might induce a person to *leave* such a group?

E. Mental Illness

1. Description

  a. Enroth alleges that a "significant number" of the youth who join cults have psychological problems as a result.[280]

  b. What Enroth claims is especially disturbing is:

  "... the fact that young people who have no history of mental pathology, and who have relatively normal, healthy personalities upon entering cultic groups, suffer the destructive impact of a very real, very frightening form of thought control or brainwashing that subjugates the will and stifles independent thinking. There is increasing clinical evidence from the various behavioral sciences for the existence of a syndrome of seduction in mental subversion involving cult converts."[281]

  c. Likewise, Steven Hassan claims that "destructive cults" can cause significant psychological damage.[282]

2. Alleged Examples

  a. Some studies purport that about one-third to one-half of those involved in destructive cults suffer some psychological harm.[283]

---

[278]Bromley and Shupe, *Strange Gods*, 111.

[279]Enroth, *Youth, Brainwashing, and the Extremist Cults*, 160.

[280]Ibid., 154-55.

[281]Ibid., 156. In a more recent article, Paul Martin concurs with this opinion. See Paul R. Martin, "Dispelling the Myths: The Psychological Consequences of Cultic Involvement," *Christian Research Journal* (Winter/Spring 1989): 11.

[282]Hassan, *Combatting Cult Mind Control*, 190ff.

[283]Martin, "Counseling the Former Cultist," 272, n. 4.

    b. Dr. John G. Clark, a psychiatrist at Harvard Medical School and Massachusetts General Hospital, spent several years studying the effects of cult membership on mental and physical health and concluded that approximately 58 percent of the cult members surveyed have chronic emotional or personality problems of a pathological nature.[284]

3. Qualifications to the Above Description

    a. Several psychological studies done on current and ex-cult members do not show a significantly greater incidence of mental illness than in the population at large.[285]

        (1) Ungerleider did not perceive people who joined cults to have been psychiatrically impaired.[286]

        (2) According to an article appearing in the *American Journal of Psychiatry,* psychiatrist J. Thomas studied 50 members and ex-members of cults and concluded: "No data emerged from intellectual, personality, or mental status testing to suggest that any of these subjects are unable or even limited in their ability to make sound judgments and legal decisions related to their persons and property."[287]

    b. Anecdotal interviews of dysfunctional ex-members can be misleading.

        (1) Some researchers draw conclusions based on interviews with ex-cultists who have left the group on negative terms.

        Because they limit their study to the "problem cases," their sample is skewed and therefore may not reflect accurately on such groups as a whole.

        (2) As Richardson cautions, "Some therapists have used therapy as a data-gathering opportunity for such case studies and have risked compromising the integrity of both endeavors. Nearly all such research is focused on ex-members whose membership or withdrawal from the group was problematic."[288]

        (3) About such skewed methodology Richardson concludes, "To treat this situation as a valid data-gathering situation is somewhat analogous to doing research on something by interview-

[284]Enroth, *Youth, Brainwashing, and the Extremist Cults*, 154-55.

[285]See, for example, Anthony and Robbins, "Law, Social Science and the 'Brainwashing' Exception," 18, 23; Richardson, "Conversion, Brainwashing, and Deprogramming," 39-40; Bromley and Shupe, *Strange Gods*, 114; Shupe and Bromley, *The New Vigilantes*, 79-80; Melton, *Encyclopedic Handbook of Cults in America*, 17.

[286]Shupe and Bromley, *The New Vigilantes*, 80.

[287]Ungerleider and Wellisch, cited in Bromley and Shupe, *Strange Gods*, 114.

[288]Richardson, "Conversion, Brainwashing, and Deprogramming," 39-40.

ing oneself over and over. The comments may be brilliant and insightful, but the data base is plainly a bit limited."[289]

(4) Any social group will have dysfunctional members.

As Anthony and Robbins state, "dysfunctionality in social groups is such a generic problem that it seems rather unlikely that 'cults' are really qualitatively different from dysfunctional families, corporate bureaucracies, youth gangs, racial prejudice and the paralyzing 'culture of poverty.'"[290]

F. *Unusual Degree of Commitment and Zeal*

1. Description

   a. Cult members are well known for their zealous dedication to the cult.[291]

   b. Cultists often put in long hours of witnessing, producing literature, and fundraising for the cult.[292]

   c. Hoekema points out that the cults make much more effective use of printed material than orthodox denominations.[293]

2. Examples

   a. Mormonism

      (1) Mormon teenagers typically dedicate two years of missionary service for the church.

      (2) Mormons also engage in massive literature distribution.

      (3) Mormons tithe generously to their church. Every day, the Mormon church brings in three million dollars in tithes.

   b. Jehovah's Witnesses

      (1) Jehovah's Witnesses are particularly well known for their zealous proselytizing.

      (2) The average practicing Jehovah's Witness spends over two hundred hours witnessing per year.[294]

      (3) The Watchtower also produces an incredible flood of literature each year.[295]

3. Qualifications to the Above Description

   a. We must be careful about comparing cultic zeal to the zeal we Christians should have for our faith.

---

[289]James T. Richardson, "The Psychology of Induction: A Review and Interpretation," in Marc Galanter, *Cults and New Religious Movements* (Washington, DC: American Psychiatric Association, 1989), 230-31.

[290]Anthony and Robbins, "Law, Social Science and the 'Brainwashing' Exception," 23.

[291]Hoekema, *The Four Major Cults*, 6.

[292]Ibid., 3. Some examples are given in the statistics section, Part II, section II.

[293]Ibid.

[294]In 1992 the figure was 239 hours per Witness.

[295]See Part II, section II.C.4.

(1) Sometimes Christians point to the cults as examples of zeal, which we ought to imitate.

For example, I have often heard Christians say that we should be as committed to evangelism as the cults are.

(2) Zeal is admirable only when it is coupled with knowledge (Rom. 10:2).

As Paul states, "It is fine to be zealous, provided the purpose is good" (Gal. 4:18).

(3) Christian zeal should flow from hearts thankful for what Christ has already done for them (Luke 7:47). Cultic zeal, on the other hand, is motivated by a desire to *earn* favor with God or to escape his judgment.

(4) Even if Christians do need to be more zealous about their faith, the cults do not provide a model for us to follow.

b. Christian groups have sometimes been called cultic for their zeal.

(1) For example, Jews for Jesus has been called a cult because of their zeal. Indeed, why would any nice Jewish boy or girl quit law school and spend the day handing out literature on the streets of New York?

(2) Campus Crusade for Christ has also been attacked for its evangelistic approach.[296]

G. Communal Lifestyle

1. Description

a. Enroth states, "The extremist cults we have studied are also, in varying degrees, communal in nature."[297]

b. Likewise, Constance Cumbey identifies communal living as "one of the pushes of the new-age movement."[298]

c. Such a lifestyle is certainly counter to American culture as a whole.

2. Examples

Examples of communal living include the Children of God, the Unification Church, some members of the Way International,[299] and the Branch Davidians.

3. Qualifications to the Above Description

a. A communal lifestyle can hardly be a hallmark of a cult when there are many Christian examples.

b. The monastic tradition in Christendom illustrates the practice of non-cultic groups living in community.

---

[296]For example, Conway and Siegelman, *Snapping*, 45.

[297]Enroth, *Youth, Brainwashing, and the Extremist Cults*, 169.

[298]Constance Cumbey, cited in Robert Passantino and Gretchen Passantino, *Witch Hunt* (Nashville: Nelson, 1990), 216.

[299]For example, some members live in "twig" homes. In Way International lingo, a "twig" refers to a small, local group of members.

    c. Certain orthodox Protestant Christian groups such as the Jesus People USA (JPUSA) in the Chicago area voluntarily live in community.

        (1) By pooling resources, their model Christian community is able to live modestly and to have an incredibly effective outreach to the inner city.

        (2) Not only is JPUSA thoroughly orthodox in its theology, but sociologically it manifests no cultic or abusive characteristics whatever.[300]

        (3) In fact, JPUSA heads up a major, well-respected counter-cult ministry.

H. Paranoia or Persecution Complex

  1. Description

    a. Walter Martin mentions the martyr or persecution complex some cultists develop.[301] Such cultists tend to regard any opposition to their teaching as a personal attack.

    b. Enroth explains the purpose such an attitude can serve: "Persecution, imagined or real, tends to unify people. In the cults a sense of belonging is enhanced and commitment strengthened by what is perceived to be persecution."[302]

  2. Examples

    a. Jehovah's Witnesses

        (1) When someone will not let them in to share their doctrinal wares, Jehovah's Witnesses regard this as persecution against Jehovah's chosen organization.

        (2) Walter Martin points out that the Jehovah's Witnesses are trained to assume that Christians hate them on a personal level. This leads to the "somewhat heroic feeling" that they are standing against "the devil's organization."[303]

        (3) Martin laments that some Christians do treat Jehovah's Witnesses rudely, thus reinforcing the Watchtower notion that all Christians hate them.

    b. Mormonism—Mormons claim that they have been singled out for persecution throughout their history.[304]

---

[300]See Timothy Jones, "Jesus' People: Lessons for Living in the 'We' Decade," *Christianity Today* (14 September 1992): 20-25.

[301]Martin, *Kingdom of the Cults*, 34.

[302]Enroth, *Youth, Brainwashing, and the Extremist Cults*, 178.

[303]Martin, *Kingdom of the Cults*, 34.

[304]See, for example, James B. Allen and Glen M. Leonard, *The Story of the Latter-day Saints*, 2d ed. (1976; rev. and enlarged, Salt Lake City: Deseret Book Company, 1992).

3. Qualifications to the Above Description

   a. Sometimes cultists really are persecuted.

      (1) Cultists are not paranoid in cases where there is genuine opposition to them.

      (2) While some illegal activity by David Koresh and his followers appears likely (e.g., pedophilia), one cannot automatically rule out anti-religious sentiments on the part of Attorney General Janet Reno's office.

      The jury is still out (literally) on the botched Bureau of Alcohol, Tobacco, and Firearms raid on the Branch Davidian compound.

      (3) Cults such as the Unification Church have been the target of deprogrammers, who have illegally kidnapped Unification Church members and thus violated their civil rights. Therefore, it is not paranoia that prompts the Unification Church to take extra precautions against such kidnappings.

   b. Sometimes Christians unwittingly feed this complex.

      (1) As Walter Martin has pointed out, Christians often slam the door and pull the shades when Jehovah's Witnesses come to their door, thus feeding the Watchtower view that they are persecuted for the kingdom.

      (2) The best way to contradict the Watchtower stereotype of Christians is to invite Witnesses in and lovingly present the gospel to them.

I. *Physical Violence*

1. Description

   a. Some cults have engaged in violent acts.[305]

   b. Enroth states, "A number of parents have experienced physical violence at the hands of cult members."[306]

   c. Since the tragic Jonestown massacre in 1978, the public has had a much greater tendency to associate violent behavior with the cults.

2. Examples

   a. Jim Jones and the People's Temple

      (1) The mass suicide of 912 people at Jonestown is one of the most well-known instances of cultic violence.[307]

      (2) Even before the mass suicide, extreme forms of "discipline" took place against young and old alike.

---

[305]Tucker, *Another Gospel*, 23.

[306]Enroth, *Youth, Brainwashing, and the Extremist Cults*, 188.

[307]An interesting general treatment of the Jonestown massacre is Marshall Kilduff and Ron Javers, *The Suicide Cult: The Inside Story of the People's Temple Sect and the Massacre in Guyana* (New York: Bantam, 1978).

In fact, in the San Francisco temple Jones set up a boxing ring to be used in exercising this discipline.[308]

   b. David Koresh and the Branch Davidians

      (1) Koresh's violent tendencies were evident even before the fire-fight with the government agents.

      (2) In 1987 a power struggle over leadership of the group ended in a gun battle.[309]

      (3) According to the testimony of ex-members, it also appears that children were beaten savagely in the name of discipline.[310]

  3. Qualifications to the Above Description

    a. Violence does not characterize most cults—especially the larger ones.

    As sociologists Bromley and Shupe point out, the Jonestown situation was a "freak event."[311]

    b. One must be careful not to generalize anecdotal stories.

      (1) The fallacy of hasty generalization becomes apparent here.

      Enroth states, "a number of parents" have experienced violence by cultists. How many are "a number of"? Is this number statistically significant? Enroth does not say.

      (2) Undoubtedly there are "a number of doctors" who "have experienced physical violence at the hands of pro-lifers." Yet, rational members of the pro-life community (including the majority of Christians) rightly resent news media efforts to generalize such actions to all pro-lifers.

J. Familial Imagery

  1. Description

    a. "One reason that young people join cults is to find a family."[312]

    b. The cult seeks to enhance commitment by replacing the person's earthly family with a new "spiritual" one.

    c. Many cults use family imagery, including references to cult members as "brothers" and "sisters," and ascribing parental titles to cult leaders.

---

[308]Sparks, *The Mindbenders*, 282.

[309]Abanes, "The Branch Davidians," 3.

[310]Samples, de Castro, Abanes, and Lyle, 58.

[311]Bromley and Shupe, *Strange Gods*, 189-90. Melton also has an excellent, balanced section on violence in cults in *Encyclopedic Handbook of Cults in America*, 361–91.

[312]Ervin Doress and Jack Nusan Porter, "Kids in Cults," in *In Gods We Trust*, 297.

2. Examples
   a. Unification Church
      (1) The Unification Church constantly talks about how the American family is degenerating into corruption while their church works toward a "perfect family."
      (2) Unification Church members regard Moon and his wife as the "True Parents."
   b. Love Family, the Family, Love Israel, Children of God
      Note the family imagery conjured up in the very titles of these cults.
3. Qualifications to the Above Description
   a. Christians use familial language. For example, Christians call one another "brother" and "sister."
   b. The Bible uses familial imagery to describe Christians' relationship to God and Christ (Mark 3:34; Luke 8:21; John 1:12; Rom. 8:3, 29; Gal. 4:1–7; Eph. 1:3–5; Heb. 2:11) and to one another (Matt. 23:8; John 21:23; 1 Cor. 6:8; Gal. 4:31; 1 Tim. 1:2; 5:1–2; 6:2; 1 Peter 3:8).

K. Distortion of Human Sexuality

1. Description
   a. "One of the hallmarks of false religion is the corruption and distortion of human sexuality."[313]
   b. This is manifested either in excess or in deprivation.
2. Examples
   a. Mormonism
      (1) The practice of polygamy illustrates the sexual excesses of the early Mormon founders and of some "fundamentalist" Mormon groups today.
      (2) Joseph Smith had twenty-seven wives and Brigham Young had fifty-three.[314]
   b. Children of God
      (1) The Children of God cult provides an example of extreme preoccupation with sex.[315]
      (2) Moses David was obsessed with the subject, as evidenced by many of his so-called Mo letters (pamphlets written for his followers and to evangelize those outside the group). The Mo letters frequently talk about sex and often contain sexually explicit artwork.

---

[313]Ronald Enroth, *The Lure of the Cults* (New York: Christian Herald Books, 1979), 83.

[314]Tanner, *The Changing World of Mormonism*, 231-33.

[315]Martin, *The New Cults*, 165-77.

      (3) The Children of God even engaged in prostitution as a means of evangelism—an activity that they termed "flirty fishing."[316]

  c. Branch Davidians

      (1) Based on a 1989 "revelation," David Koresh decreed that all females in the commune belonged to him, including the married women.

      (2) Some of Koresh's "wives" were only twelve years old.[317]

  3. Qualifications to the Above Description

    a. This particular sin does not characterize all cults.

    b. The recent scandals involving well-known evangelical "celebrities" graphically reveal that cults do not have a corner on this vice.

L. Antagonism Toward Orthodox Christian Denominations

  1. Description

    a. "All cults view themselves as being independent and identify themselves in opposition to other bodies."[318]

    b. Cults sometimes expend considerable energy denouncing other religious groups—particularly Christian churches.[319]

    c. Though the cults have little in common with one another, they share a common opposition to Christians.

  2. Examples

    a. Mormonism

      (1) Mormons regard their religion as a "restoration" of true Christianity, which was "lost" early in the history of the church.

      (2) In his initial visions, Joseph Smith allegedly was told not to join any of the denominations because "they were all wrong," "their creeds were an abomination in his [God's] sight," and their adherents were "all corrupt."[320]

      (3) Speaking of Christianity outside of Mormonism, John Taylor stated, "It is as corrupt as hell; and the Devil could not invent a better engine to spread his work."[321]

    b. Jehovah's Witnesses

      (1) Charles Taze Russell, the founder of the Jehovah's Witnesses, engaged in tireless, blistering denunciations against the "apostate" clergy of "Christendom"—Catholic and Protestant alike.

---

[316]Deborah (Linda Berg) Davis, *The Children of God: The Inside Story* (Grand Rapids: Zondervan, 1984), 118–19, 122–23, 136–37, 202.

[317]Abanes, "The Branch Davidians," 4. See also Samples, de Castro, Abanes, and Lyle, *Prophets of the Apocalypse,* which notes throughout the book Koresh's preoccupation with sex.

[318]Harold L. Busséll, *Unholy Devotion* (Grand Rapids: Zondervan, 1983), 59.

[319]Ronald Enroth, "Churches on the Fringe," in *Contend for the Faith*, 196.

[320]Joseph Smith 2:19, in Pearl of Great Price.

[321]Journal of Discourses 6:167.

(2) The Watchtower society continues to maintain a hostile attitude toward so-called apostate Christendom.

c. Herbert W. Armstrong

(1) Armstrong attacked the denominations of his day.

(2) In fact, Armstrong assailed the church of the previous eighteen centuries, claiming that the gospel had not been preached during that time.[322]

3. Qualifications to the Above Description

a. Genuinely Christian groups vary as to how much contact they will have with Christians outside their own denominational circle.

b. For example, certain types of fundamentalist groups may tend to avoid contact with other Christian bodies perceived to be less strict on certain doctrinal or behavioral issues.

c. In the case of cults this antagonism is usually carried to an extreme.

M. Opposition Toward Autonomous Thinking

1. Description

a. Some cults discourage autonomous thinking.

b. This opposition relates to the cult's authoritarian character. If the cult possesses "the truth," to question its teaching is to question God himself.[323]

2. Examples

a. Jehovah's Witnesses

(1) The Jehovah's Witnesses discourage independent thought. Any Witness who questions the Watchtower position runs the risk of being "disfellowshipped."

(2) When Raymond Franz, nephew of then Watchtower president Frederick Franz, questioned the Watchtower teaching about the number of "born again" Christians being limited to 144,000,[324] he and several others were disfellowshipped for disloyalty to the organization.

b. Christian Science

(1) Christian Scientists typically do not study the Bible on their own.

---

[322]Herbert W. Armstrong, *The Autobiography of Herbert W. Armstrong*, 2 vols. (Pasadena: Ambassador College Press, 1967), 1:502-3. Interestingly, the Worldwide Church seems to be softening its hostility toward Christian groups. For example, the February 1994 *Plain Truth* ran a very favorable story about the Salvation Army.

[323]On the authoritarian character of cults, see point A above.

[324]Robert M. Bowman, Jr. discusses the doctrine of the 144,000 in the Jehovah's Witness volume in this series.

      (2) Rather, whenever they do read the Bible it is in the context of Mary Baker Eddy's explanation of it (e.g., in *Science and Health with Key to the Scriptures*).

  3. Qualifications to the Above Description

     a. Cultists may be *discouraged* from thinking autonomously, but this does not mean that they absolutely lose their ability to do so.[325]

     b. Many legitimate Christian organizations limit autonomous thinking in certain respects.

      (1) For example, some have doctrinal statements or confessions of faith that professors, pastors, and others must sign.

        In signing these, pastors or professors agree that their beliefs fall within the guidelines of the denomination or school's statement of faith.

      (2) Most schools, churches, and denominations allow flexibility within the guidelines of their statement of faith. In cultic situations, autonomous thought may be regimented to an extreme, even on minute points.

N. *Fraud and Deception*

  1. Description

     a. In the popular media, fraudulent and deceptive practices are often associated with cults.

     b. In some cases the deception involves the cult's failure to disclose its true identity to prospective converts and donors.[326]

     c. Some argue that cults perpetrate fraud even when they do reveal their true identity.

      (1) Some say that cults should warn people (especially young people) up front about problems they may experience as a result of their involvement with the group.

      (2) For example, the cult should warn people that by dedicating their life to the cult they may not develop marketable skills, may experience emotional problems, etc.

  2. Examples

     a. Unification Church

      (1) The Unification Church is often cited as the classic example of a deceptive cult, particularly in recruiting and fundraising.

      (2) "Heavenly Deception"

        (a) The doctrine of "heavenly deception" is the Unification Church teaching that lying is permissible if it furthers the kingdom of God (i.e., the work of the Unification Church).

---

[325]As noted in section III.E above, cultists are not mind controlled or brainwashed.

[326]Tucker, *Another Gospel*, 23; Anthony and Robbins, "Law, Social Science and the 'Brainwashing' Exception," 8.

(b) Former Unification Church member Chris Elkins defines heavenly deception as "the policy of using falsehood to achieve, supposedly, goodness. The practice of employing lies for the sake of heaven. Heavenly deception is a thread that extends far into the fabric of the Unification Church."[327]

(3) J. Isamu Yamamoto, an expert on the Unification Church, relates his own experience: "On numerous occasions, I have personally observed Unificationists practice 'heavenly deception.' For example, I have encountered Unificationists in wheelchairs soliciting funds for social programs that did not exist, and when I asked them why they pretended to be disabled as they walked to their van, they used the concept of 'heavenly deception' to defend their actions."[328]

b. Hare Krishna

Members of the Krishna sect have been accused of misrepresentation when soliciting funds at airports and other public places.

3. Qualifications to the Above Description

a. It is unreasonable to demand that a cult—or any religious group— state up front all possible negative consequences that may arise from associating with it.

(1) Even legitimate, mainstream churches have members who may be dissatisfied with their experience, but we do not call such churches deceptive because they do not provide a disclosure statement.

(2) "Religious conversion cannot be handled like purchasing a washer and dryer, complete with limited warranties for parts and labor and money-back guarantee. To require a new religion to lay out for a potential convert a contract stating precisely where and what he will be doing in twenty years' time or to provide a laundry list of future subjective and material sacrifices balanced against benefits and rewards is to ask the impossible. We would consider it to be absurd if we demanded the same of conventional churches when they take in converts."[329]

b. Sometimes complaints about deception are actually expressions of disapproval toward the group's beliefs and practices.

(1) "One barrier to generalizing the notion of cultic 'deception' beyond the concealment of a group's identity may be the increasing entanglement of claims about deception and damage with implicit derogation of the validity of religious doctrine.

---

[327]Chris Elkins, *Heavenly Deception* (Wheaton, Ill.: Tyndale House, 1980), 14.

[328]See the Unification Church volume in this series.

[329]Bromley and Shupe, *Strange Gods*, 106.

It is difficult to separate evaluation of the effects of belief . . . from evaluation of the belief itself."[330]

(2) Consider the well-known film "The God Makers," a popular anti-Mormon film produced by evangelical Christians.[331]

The film is cast as a "docudrama," in which the protagonist seeks legal recourse against "fraud" and "misrepresentation" by the Mormon church. The fraud allegedly perpetrated is that the Mormon church claims to be Christian when in fact it is not. The majority of the film is spent demonstrating the anti-Christian nature of Mormonism. The film ends with the lawyers agreeing that the would-be plaintiff certainly could win his case were it not for the power and influence of the Mormon church. Now, assuming the makers of this film are serious, the last thing Christians should desire is to have our judicial system evaluate theological truth claims for "fraud"!

---

[330]Anthony and Robbins, "Law, Social Science and the 'Brainwashing' Exception," 11.

[331]I.e., Jeremiah Films.

Part V: Why Do People Join Cults?

I. General Observations

A. Personal Needs

1. Robert and Gretchen Passantino, who have done cult apologetics for over twenty years, note that "a person usually joins a cult because he has problems that he is having trouble solving, and the cult promises to solve these problems."[332]

2. Doress and Porter, authors of an article entitled "Kids in Cults," observe that "whatever needs brought them in (security, rebellion, recognition, idealism) will also make them stay."[333]

3. While some cults meet—or *appear* to meet—the needs of many of their followers, the Passantinos caution that the cults cannot truly and permanently meet the needs that only the gospel can fulfill:

   "[People who become involved in cults] think that the cult can meet those needs. Cults always offer to meet such personal needs, and they may appear to meet those needs for a while, but since the cults are only counterfeits of the true gospel, they ultimately leave the cult follower with the same unfulfilled needs."[334]

4. Kurt Van Gorden identifies four categories of needs that people seek to meet by joining cults: intellectual, emotional, social, and spiritual.[335]

5. There is nothing cultic about the needs themselves; all people have them in varying degrees.

6. Note, too, that the reasons mentioned above are also reasons people turn to Christ.

B. Doctrinal Reasons Rarely a Factor

1. While it would be an overstatement to say that no one joins a cult for doctrinal reasons, it does appear that relatively few people do.

---

[332]Robert Passantino and Gretchen Passantino, *Answers to the Cultist at Your Door* (Eugene, Ore.: Harvest House, 1981), 22.

[333]Doress and Porter, "Kids in Cults," 300-301.

[334]Passantino and Passantino, *Answers to the Cultist,* 13.

[335]Kurt Van Gorden, "Unity School of Christianity," in *Evangelizing the Cults,* 140.

2. "A person does not usually join a cult because he has done an exhaustive analysis of world religions and has decided that a particular cult presents the best theology available."[336]

3. For example, "joining the Mormons often happens before the new convert has a clear idea of everything Mormons believe."[337]

C. Unfulfilled Expectations in Traditional Churches

1. The Passantinos observe that "people start and join cults because they have personal needs that aren't being met in traditional churches."

2. Recall that three-quarters of all newly baptized Mormons are former Protestants.[338]

3. Van Baalen calls the cults "the unpaid bills of the church," meaning that in those areas where the church has been ineffective or "lopsided," the cults have rushed in to fill the vacuum.[339]

   a. J. Gordon Melton, a member of the United Methodist Church, concurs with Van Baalen. He believes that the impersonality of many Christian churches contributes to the increase in cult membership.

   b. Melton notes that the cults tend to do best with young people who do not feel like they fit in with the mainline churches.[340]

4. We must be careful, however, not to overstate the church's failure.

   a. Michael Langone raises a valid criticism: "It is unfair to condemn mainline religions for 'failing' to fulfill spiritual needs because (1) they are often competing against 'cheats' who manipulate rather than respect the religious seeker and (2) in today's secular climate it is unrealistic to hold mainline religions responsible for the spiritual fulfillment of their members. The individual must bear primary responsibility for him or herself."[341]

   b. In one sense Langone is correct: the church cannot *make* people be happy or spiritual; personal responsibility is also key.

   c. It is the church's responsibility, however, to attend to the spiritual, emotional, social, and even physical well-being of its members, which it has not always done.

---

[336]Passantino and Passantino, *Answers to the Cultist*, 22.

[337]Allan, *Shopping for a God*, 109.

[338]See statistics in Part II, section II.B.2.c.

[339]Van Baalen, *Chaos of the Cults*, 390. See also Martin, *Kingdom of the Cults*, 14.

[340]Tucker, *Another Gospel*, 26.

[341]Michael Langone, "Treatment of Individuals and Families Troubled by Cult Involvement," *Update. A Quarterly Journal on New Religious Movements* 7, no. 1 (March 1983): 27-39.

II. Needs People Seek to Meet Through Cults

A. Love

1. As Richardson observes, "People affiliate with groups because they want affection; they want friends and loved ones to care for them."[342]

2. The need for loving, personal relationships applies to many different groups, religious and non-religious.

   a. Doress states, "Loving relationships will tend to sustain them and make them want to remain in the institution. This is one of the reasons that cults are difficult to fight—they are hard to replace in this crucial area of loving care. People will not leave unless the cult changes or they begin to see the true nature of it, i.e., that it is *not* so loving and caring after all."[343]

   b. People are attracted to the Unity School of Christianity[344] because of their emphasis on love: how to love yourself, how to love other people, etc.[345]

   c. Unification Church members used to practice what some have pejoratively called "love bombing" at their introductory retreats. The prospective convert was showered with compliments, expressions of personal interest, etc.[346]

B. Family

1. "One reason that young people join cults is to find a family."[347]

2. Doress and Porter cite factors such as divorce, generational conflicts between parent and child, and child abuse as motivators for some young people to seek a new family in a cult.[348]

3. For example, the Unification Church constantly talks about how the American family is degenerating into corruption while they work toward attaining the "perfect family."[349]

4. Cults often invoke familial imagery, sometimes in the very name of the group (e.g., the Love Family, the Family, Love Israel).[350]

---

[342]Richardson, "Conversion, Brainwashing, and Deprogramming," 37.

[343]Doress and Porter, "Kids in Cults," 300.

[344]Not to be confused with Unitarianism, which is also a cult. (See Part III, section II.I.2.c.)

[345]McDowell and Stewart, *The Deceivers,* 18.

[346]Bromley and Shupe discuss this practice in *Strange Gods,* 121. Note that the expression "love bombing" is a loaded term, implying that the expressions of love are a ruse. Perhaps in some instances they were, but this cannot be assumed. It seems prejudicial to accuse the Moonies of "love bombing" when similar expressions of love and personal interest practiced by a conventional religion would be seen as evidence of a "caring" church. Regardless, the Unification Church dropped the practice in the early 1980s and are now more reserved in their displays of affection toward potential converts.

[347]Doress and Porter, "Kids in Cults," 297.

[348]Ibid., 298.

[349]Ibid., 297.

[350]On the use of familial imagery see Part IV, section IV.J.

C. Acceptance and Self-Worth

1. People who feel like they "don't belong" in society can be especially vulnerable to cultic involvement.

2. Solomon notes, "Decisions among today's youth to join groups like the Unification church can, in large measure, be explained by the intensification of feelings of alienation and isolation."[351]

3. "Many groups have flourished because they were able to offer a sense of worth and identity to people who lacked it."[352]

4. Since most cults make spectacular claims about their importance in the divine order, cult members feel as though they are participating in something special and are on "God's side."

5. Cults tend to give a significant role to the laity, thus elevating the importance of the individual member.

   a. Consider Mormonism, with its emphasis on the "priesthood" and the two years that Mormon young people devote to mission work.

   b. Jehovah's Witnesses also mobilize their members, who go door to door spreading the Watchtower's gospel of the kingdom.

   c. Hoekema asks, "Are the established churches using their laymen to the best advantage? Or are we missing some real opportunities here?"[353]

D. Idealism

1. Allan speaks of the idealism that typifies many people who join cults.[354]

2. "Christians must confess that often they have been impassive to the economically and socially needy, the suffering, the sorrowing, the unsaved. The enthusiasm and the sacrifice of the cults shame us. Their educational vision and their extensive use of modern methods of propagandizing the masses have left many of us far behind."[355]

3. For example, The People's Temple was involved in many works of philanthropy and charity, such as running nursing homes, adopting unwanted children, etc.[356]

   Some who were involved with Jim Jones really were not interested in the religious aspect at all, but simply in the social programs he spearheaded.[357]

E. Spiritual Fulfillment

1. People sometimes join cults to satisfy their spiritual hunger.

---

[351]Solomon, "Integrating the 'Moonie' Experience," 293.
[352]Allan, *Shopping for a God*, 37.
[353]Hoekema, *The Four Major Cults*, 5-6.
[354]Allan, *Shopping for a God*, 113.
[355]Lewis, *Confronting the Cults*, 9.
[356]Sparks, *The Mindbenders*, 275.
[357]Ibid., 271.

2. Even as our society has become more secular, in some ways it has become more "spiritual."

   a. Unfortunately, some of the spirituality is of a counterfeit sort.

   b. For example, the New Age movement has tapped into this spiritual hunger, but feeds its adherents a diet of monism, pantheism, and self-deification.[358]

3. The cults claim to offer spiritual fulfillment by following their teaching and adhering to their regimen.

F. Answers to Intellectual Questions

1. Sometimes people—and especially young people—look to cults in their search for answers.

2. Van Baalen cites the Jehovah's Witnesses as an example.[359]

   a. The Witnesses speak authoritatively and powerfully, claiming to believe the Bible without reservation.

   b. They also present a veneer of scholarship, invoking arguments from Greek, Hebrew, church history, etc.

   c. A person seeking answers can easily be taken in by such an authoritative display.

3. Victor Paul Wierwille's Way International cult has attracted some because of his impression of profound scholarship (e.g., his use of Aramaic and Greek).[360]

G. Wholesome Lifestyle

1. No doubt some people who join cults experience an immediate improvement in their lifestyles.

2. For example, an undisciplined person strung out on drugs may actually benefit from the cult's regimen and discipline.

3. Busséll points out that sometimes even Christians become involved in cultic groups because the cultic lifestyle can be very clean-cut.

   a. Because certain Christian denominations define holiness in terms of "dos" and "don'ts," a person brought up in such denominations may assume that a particular cult is fine because it observes the same wholesome lifestyle.

   b. For example, some Christian groups confuse avoiding certain cultural practices—such as smoking, drinking, and dancing—with true holiness. On this basis the Mormon lifestyle may appear to be truly "holy" because they, too, abstain from alcohol, tobacco, and even caffeine.[361]

---

[358]"Monism" is the teaching that all reality is ultimately one. Pantheism is the teaching that all is God. Self-deification is the teaching that since all is one and all is God, we too are God.

[359]Van Baalen, *Chaos of the Cults,* 392.

[360]McDowell and Stewart, *The Deceivers,* 17.

[361]Busséll, *Unholy Devotion,* 73.

Part VI:
Keeping People Out of the Cults

It has been well said that it is better to build a fence at the top of a cliff than to run an ambulance service at the bottom. With that in mind, let us consider some *preventive* measures that can keep people from joining cults in the first place. While the principles listed below are no *guarantee,* their practice can greatly decrease the likelihood that our church and family members will turn to the cults.

I. Cult-Proofing Your Church

A. *The Christian church should learn from the cults.*
   1. Christians might assume that because the cults are heretical there is nothing we can learn from them, but such an idea is dangerously false.
   2. Christians admit that we can learn a great deal about what *not* to do from the cults. But the cults would not be attractive if they did not offer (or at least *seem* to offer) what many people are seeking.
   3. Since the cults capitalize on the weak areas of the church and seem to offer an alternative, by examining carefully those areas in which the cults experience the greatest success we may be able to learn how to strengthen our churches.
   4. Since most people join cults because of legitimate needs in their lives,[362] the church should seek to meet those needs.

      Neff asks pointedly, "Why have these people found answers to their needs in cults and new religions rather than in the Christian church? Can the church listen to what cult members are saying and, in turn, show them how Jesus meets their needs?"[363]
   5. If we keep in mind that people join cults because of intellectual, social, emotional, and spiritual needs, we can offer true fulfillment by practicing vibrant, biblical Christianity in our churches.

---

[362]See the extensive discussion throughout Part V on the needs people seek to meet through cult involvement.

[363]LaVonne Neff, "Evaluating Cults and New Religions," in *A Guide to Cults and New Religions,* 197-98.

B. We need to meet our church members' intellectual needs.

1. Christians need to know what they believe and why they believe it.

   a. Walter Martin used to complain that many Christians knew what they believed but not why they believe it. In my opinion there are an increasing number of Christians who know neither.

   b. Christians need to be rooted in the essentials of the faith.

      (1) Every Christian should be able to state accurately the doctrine of the Trinity, the deity of Christ, the bodily resurrection, and salvation by grace through faith alone.

      (2) Every Christian should be able to defend these doctrines from Scripture.

   c. When Christians cannot articulate and defend their doctrine they are easy prey for the cults.

      (1) As Walter Martin used to say, "It is a sad fact that a ninety-day [i.e., newly trained] wonder from the Watchtower Bible and Tract Society can turn the average Christian into a doctrinal pretzel in fifteen minutes."

      (2) Not a few Christians have been sucked into cultic groups because they were not grounded in the fundamentals of Scripture.

   d. When Christians know the "real thing," they will not be fooled by counterfeits.

      (1) Bank tellers are trained to detect counterfeit money by carefully studying real money. They become so familiar with the genuine article that when a fake bill comes through they can detect it instantly.

      (2) Similarly, the single most important thing a Christian can do to deal with cultic error is to thoroughly know the truth.

         It is not necessary for Christians to learn about every cult under the sun (though some teaching on cultic beliefs is certainly helpful; see point 3 below).

   e. A church that spends all (or even most) of its time teaching on recovery, self-esteem, codependency, getting to know one's "inner child," etc., should not be surprised when a cultist destroys some member's faith.

   f. The church has a divine command to "preach the word . . . with all longsuffering and doctrine" (2 Tim. 4:2, KJV). It ignores this command only at its peril.

2. We need to take people's intellectual questions about the faith seriously and strive to provide serious answers.

   a. Sometimes when Christians are faced with questions they cannot answer they shift into "piety mode."

b. For example, a person was recounting her experience of witnessing to a Muslim. When the Muslim asked her to explain how God could be both one and three she was unable to respond. A well-meaning Christian counseled her to tell the Muslim, "The Trinity is something you need to believe on faith. You need to pray about it and God will reveal it to you."

c. There are several problems with the above counsel.

    (1) This answer, in effect, says, "The doctrine of the Trinity makes no sense and is indefensible logically and theologically. Nevertheless, you need to believe it on blind faith."

    (2) It is no different from the "burning in the bosom" answer of Mormonism.[364]

    (3) It ignores the command, "Always be prepared to give an answer to everyone who asks you to give the reason for the hope that you have" (1 Peter 3:15).

d. Fortunately, instead of following this counsel, the Christian read some books on the Trinity. This not only prepared her for her next witnessing encounter but also strengthened her faith.

3. Churches should teach classes on the cults.

a. Though the church should focus on teaching Christian doctrine generally, it is helpful to teach periodically on what the cults (and other religions) believe and why.

b. This teaching can equip Christians to know how to witness to cultists.

c. Teaching on the cults also strengthens our faith as we consider how to answer cultic objections. We hold our convictions more firmly when forced to defend them.

4. Churches need to teach people to think critically.

a. It is not enough for us to tell Christians what they should believe about this or that doctrine. Christians need to understand *principles* for discerning truth from error.

b. Many Christians are exceedingly gullible and undiscerning.

    (1) Christians have been willing to believe everything from claims that scientists in Siberia drilled a hole so deep that they discovered hell,[365] to wild, incredible, unsubstantiated stories of large-scale Satanic ritual abuse.[366]

---

[364]See part III, section II.J.2.a.

[365]Rich Buhler, *The Great Christian Rumors* (Costa Mesa, Calif.: Branches Communications, 1991), 14-20.

[366]Robert Passantino and Gretchen Passantino, "The Hard Facts about Satanic Ritual Abuse," *Christian Research Journal* (Winter 1992); Robert Passantino, Gretchen Passantino, and John Trott, "Satan's Sideshow," *Cornerstone* vol. 18, issue 90; Leon Jaroff, "Lies of the Mind," *Time* (29 November 1993): 52-59. See also the Satanism volume in this series.

(2) When Christians do not understand how to evaluate evidence and how to detect blatant fallacies in reasoning, they are "infants, tossed back and forth by the waves, and blown here and there by every wind of teaching" (Eph. 4:14).

c. If Christians are to be people who love the truth (1 Cor. 13:6; 2 Thess. 2:10), they cannot afford to engage in sloppy thinking.

d. An outstanding book on this subject is *Witch Hunt*, by Bob and Gretchen Passantino.

C. We need to meet our people's social and emotional needs.

1. Though the church is not a social club, it nevertheless should be a place where people can develop meaningful friendships.

2. Melton points out that quite a few people who leave mainline churches for cults do so because the church seems cold and impersonal.[367]

   The cults especially attract young people who feel they do not fit in the conventional church.

3. Churches should be programmatic in providing opportunities for fellowship.

   Small group situations, which allow for intimacy not possible in the larger church setting, can be very important in counteracting anonymity and impersonality in our churches.

4. Church leaders need to set the tone.

   a. Hospitality is important (Rom. 12:13; 16:23; 1 Tim. 5:10; 1 Peter 4:9; 3 John 8).

   b. As we open our homes and our hearts to others they may feel less need to look elsewhere for caring relationships.

D. We need to meet our church members' spiritual needs.

1. The cults capitalize on instances of hypocrisy in the church, claiming to promote true, zealous, "sold-out" spirituality.

2. The cults have zeal, but without true knowledge (Rom. 10:2).

   a. There are genuine Christian churches that have true knowledge but little zeal (i.e., they are God's "frozen" people).

   b. The biblical balance is zeal *with* understanding (2 Peter 1:3–8).

3. To meet our church member's spiritual needs it is necessary to feed them a steady diet of true doctrine from the Bible (1 Peter 2:2; 2 Tim. 3:16).

4. We must also cultivate an attractive atmosphere of worship that addresses heart and head alike.

5. The above recommendations are things churches should do even if there were no cults; they are an important part of a healthy, vibrant

---

[367]Melton, cited in Tucker, *Another Gospel*, 26.

church. But it is also true that a healthy church is the best weapon against losing people to cults.

II. Cult-Proofing Your Children

While the suggestions given below are not foolproof, they can go a long way toward making our children less susceptible to involvement in a cult.

A. A strong family is a key to keeping your kids away from the cults.[368]

1. Young people need the security and stability of a loving, supportive family. If they do not find this at home they may seek it in a cult.[369]

2. There are certain family problems that can make a young person especially prone to cultic involvement. These are discussed in points B-E below.

B. Keep open the lines of communication.

1. Talk openly with your kids about *whatever* they want to discuss, including "non-spiritual" issues.

   a. If you generally have good communication with your child then talking to him or her about spiritual issues will not seem to come from out of left field.

   b. In fact, your son or daughter will become resentful if the only time you are willing to talk is when you are "preaching religion" at them.

   c. In other words, a pattern of good communication generally will set the stage for you to impart spiritual values as well.

2. Speak openly to your children about your faith.

   a. Parents and not the church are primarily responsible to bring up their children "in the training and instruction of the Lord" (Eph. 6:4).

   b. Parents ought not to expect the Sunday school teacher or pastor to shoulder all the responsibility for their child's spiritual nurturing.

   c. However, remember that speaking openly about your faith is not the same thing as forcing it down their throats.

C. Respect your son or daughter as an individual.

1. Young people need to be respected as individuals, not as clones of their parents.

2. Some young people have joined cults simply because it provided an easy way of differentiating themselves from their parents.

---

[368]Anthony and Robbins, "New Religions, Families, and 'Brainwashing,'" 269.

[369]Doress and Porter, "Kids in Cults," 298.

a. When parents do not allow their children legitimate freedom to express their personalities, children sometimes rebel by joining a cult.

b. Doress and Porter state that, according to their research, some of the young people who joined cults had already tried different forms of rebellion such as drugs, promiscuity, and running away.

   (1) In the cults they can show their differentiation from their parents through a totally different lifestyle, such as communal living, different attitudes toward money, clothing, hair, etc.

   (2) Thus, cult membership provides a way of separating themselves from their parents' value system.

c. Therefore, parents need to "pick their battles."

   (1) If children want to express themselves in ways that differ from parental values but are not inherently destructive (e.g., a particular style of dress), a wise parent will allow this freedom of expression.

   (2) Allowing legitimate freedom will serve a twofold purpose in keeping your son and daughter from a cult:

      (a) It may make the young person feel less need to rebel in the first place.

      (b) It allows the parent to express concern about potential involvement with an undesirable religious group without being perceived as harping on *everything* the young person might want to do.

3. Joining a cult also can be a way of receiving recognition, even if it is negative.

a. "The cults seem to be a short-cut method of achieving instant attention and recognition."[370]

b. Doress and Porter state, "The saffron robes of the Hare Krishna and the rough cloth robes of the Children of God are attention getting. It is a way of saying: 'Here I am, whether you like it or not. I exist. And you'd better listen, or the world will come to an end!'"[371]

c. If you are careful to affirm your son or daughter for his or her achievements and character, he or she may not feel the need to gain attention through a cult.

D. *Take your child's questions seriously, and make every effort to provide answers.*

1. At least some kids join cults in "a spiritual search for answers."[372]

---

[370]Ibid., 299.
[371]Ibid.
[372]Ibid., 298.

2. Doress and Porter observe, "Children reared in mature, established religions are used to not getting answers to their questions. This can lead to a sense of incompleteness and dissatisfaction. When a cult comes along and offers definitive and complete answers, it is very tempting for the youngsters to be caught up in the lifestyles of the answer-givers."[373]

3. Parents should admit when they do not know the answer to a biblical or theological question and seek the answer from another Christian with knowledge on the subject or from appropriate books (e.g., commentaries).

4. Do not chastise your son or daughter for asking "dangerous" questions.

   a. Sometimes young people will question whether God exists, whether the Christian faith is true, whether the Bible is the word of God, etc.

   b. The worst thing you can do is to act horrified or to take a heavy-handed, authoritarian approach.

      Do not lay a guilt trip on your son or daughter, or rebuke them for daring to ask such "blasphemous" questions.

   c. Those who work through issues for themselves will hold their convictions more firmly than those who hold them on the authority of others.

5. Provide guidance to your young person about how to think biblically, logically, and theologically (see point F below).

E. Live a consistent Christian life with your children.

1. Young people spot hypocrisy a mile away.

2. If you do not live a consistent Christian life then do not be surprised if your children reject Christianity.

   a. "Consistent" does not mean "perfect."

   b. Children learn from how you handle your failures as well as your successes.

      For example, seeking your children's forgiveness when you have wronged them can powerfully demonstrate the reality of your faith.

F. Teach your children crucial principles of discernment.

1. As noted in point I above on cult-proofing your church, it is important to teach your children how to discern truth from error.

2. It is better to teach children *principles* that they can apply on their own in new situations than simply to teach them what to believe about this or that doctrine.

---

[373]Ibid.

3. Michael Langone points out that most mainline churches fail "in teaching young people how to think critically about philosophical and religious matters."[374]

   "In my clinical and personal experience, I have encountered very intelligent individuals who are remarkably unable to challenge (not because of unassertiveness) low-grade sophistry. Perhaps the public and religious educational establishments need more gadflies to shake young people out of the nonthinking submissiveness that society rewards in so many ways."[375]

4. As concerned parents it is our responsibility to train our children to think critically; we cannot rely on our churches and educational institutions to do it.

5. Whenever possible, stress *principles* and let your kids reason through the particular issue.

   a. For example, rather than simply preaching to your children about the evils of television, Os Guinness suggests that you could play a game called "Spot the Lie."

      As you listen to the news cast, commercials, or a sit-com and are presented with philosophies and values contrary to the Christian faith, see who can spot the fallacious reasoning and faulty conclusions first.

   b. By asking your young person the right questions, you can get *them* to come to the proper conclusion. They will then internalize the truth better than if you simply preach at them.

---

[374]Langone, "Treatment of Individuals and Families," 34.
[375]Ibid.